Drawdown Survival Guide

Drawdown Survival Guide

P. J. Budahn

NAVAL INSTITUTE PRESS
Annapolis, Maryland

Library of Congress Cataloging-in-Publication Data

Budahn, P. J. (Phillip J.), 1949–
    Drawdown survival guide / P. J. Budahn.
        p.   cm.
    Includes bibliographical references and index.
    ISBN 1-55750-090-8
        1. Job hunting—United States—Handbooks, manuals, etc.
    2. Retired military personnel—Employment—United States—Handbooks,
    manuals, etc.   3. Veterans—Employment—United States—Handbooks,
    manuals, etc.   4. Pensions, Military—United States—Handbooks,
    manuals, etc.   5. Veterans—United States—Societies, etc.—
    Directories.   I. Title.
    HF5382.75.U6B83   1993
    650.14—dc20   93-1671
                                                               CIP

Printed in the United States of America on acid-free paper ∞

9 8 7 6 5 4 3 2

First printing

Table of Contents

INTRODUCTION 1

1 Emergency Inventory 3

2 Beginnings and Endings: Seven Truths for a
Successful Transition 7

3 Morale Check 17

4 Who Goes, Who Stays? 23

5 Five-Step Financial Self-Analysis 39

6 Getting Back to Work: The Networking
Connection 43

7 The Ten-Step, Two-Minute Networking Phone
Call 49

8 A Pre-Resume, Pre-Job-Search Review 51

9 The Quick-and-Dirty Job Search 59

10 Constructing Your Resume: Balloons, Building
Blocks, and Sketches 61

11 Exit Bonuses and Separation Pay 75

12 Continuing Military Benefits   107

13 On-Base Drawdown Benefits   117

14 Job-Hunting Services   135

15 For All Veterans   145

16 Your Discharge Day (D-Day) Checklist   153

APPENDIXES

A Military Pay in Civilian Dollars   173

B Sample Training Verification   174

C Typical Schedule for TAP Course   179

D National Veterans' Organizations   181

E State Veterans' Offices   183

F Drawdown Reading List   187

INDEX   191

Drawdown Survival Guide

Introduction

It's a tough time to take off the uniform. Uncertainty about the future is widespread throughout the civilian economy. Fundamental changes are under way in the kinds of work Americans do and the skills they need to do them.

Into this jumbled job market are coming hundreds of thousands of military people. They've won the Cold War. They've won the Persian Gulf War. And now it's time to go home.

Congress and the Pentagon have tried to be helpful. They have assembled a special package of benefits and programs, and added them to veterans' benefits that have been around since the end of World War II. The aim is to smooth out the path for the men and women returning to the civilian world during the military's manpower reductions of the 1990s.

Unfortunately, the new programs have become the source of frustration, confusion, and misunderstandings. Some benefits go to specific segments of the military population, and some go to everyone. Some benefits depend on the type of separation you request, and some depend on the separation the military chooses for you.

Figuring out who gets what and appreciating the legal fine print takes time. That's time that can be better spent preparing for a new job or looking for a new home.

Drawdown Survival Guide is a tool for everyone leaving active duty and everyone contemplating a change. It summarizes the major benefits and programs, in clear, simple English, with emphasis upon identifying the specific groups of military people who are eligible for each benefit.

The book was written with the spouses of military people in mind. In many households, the spouse is the person who manages the family budget and attends to the myriad details of closing up one home, finding another, and getting the family from here to there. *Drawdown Survival Guide* is spouse-friendly.

At the back of the book are charts and lists with all sorts of useful information for people coming off active duty. Before going further with this book, you might want to glance at the chapter entitled "Your Discharge Day (D-Day) Checklist." The checklist reminds you what to do, when to do it, and who to see.

Transition benefits have been provided by a grateful nation to help military people make the adjustment back to the private sector. No one should feel squeamish or hesitant about using these benefits.

Know what you should get. And use what you can.

Emergency Inventory

A successful transition from active duty to the civilian world calls for a mixture of action and planning. Action without planning can waste precious weeks with aimless effort. Planning without action will leave a veteran with pages filled with wonderful schemes but without a job.

Before putting together a personalized blend of action and planning, you need to review your present situation. Action may be called for today, regardless of how far you are from your discharge date. You may have needs and problems that can't wait for the last weeks—or even the last six months—in uniform.

This emergency inventory follows a format that's used throughout the book. In the upper-right corner of the page is a box. On this page, the box is filled with the words "Take Action Today." But in most instances, that box will be empty. It's your job, when encountering one of those boxes, to fill in a specific date.

It's not enough to read a description of some needed action, then to mutter, "That's a good idea. I'll remember to follow through before I'm discharged."

Some transitions happen, others are managed. If you want a transition that's managed, then become your own manager. Give yourself clear, specific, achievable objectives. Fix a deadline by which the task must be accomplished. Don't rely upon memory. Every manager has stories about subordinates forgetting an important deadline or misunderstanding a perfectly clear one. Things aren't necessarily smoother when you're managing yourself. So write down all deadlines.

You also need to develop the habit of writing down dates, names, addresses, and phone numbers of contacts. You will encounter dozens of people as you leave active duty and look for work in the private sector. It's not always possible to predict who will turn out to be important, or what nugget of information will suddenly become vital.

Long after your discharge you may need to know the name of that clerk in the chaplain's office who mentioned having a brother in your hometown. Or, exactly when did you visit the family service center? How can you write to your base's judge advocate general? What was your job counselor's phone number?

You need to record those details. At the end of this "emergency inventory," space has been provided to write down the names, addresses, and phone numbers of people you contact as a result of going through this checklist, plus the date you dealt with them. Get into the habit of writing down these facts. A successful transition and job search often depend upon your mastery of the little details.

Here are some indicators that call for immediate action:

	Yes	No
Do you need more education or technical training to make your skills marketable?	___	___
Do you have a chronic medical or dental problem that can benefit from immediate medical care?	___	___

	Yes	*No*
Does a family member have a chronic medical or dental problem that would benefit from immediate care?	___	___
Could you or a family member take advantage now of an elective medical or dental procedure?	___	___
Do you or a family member need counseling for an individual or marriage problem or for substance abuse?	___	___
Would you be unable to pay your normal living expenses for at least two months—and ideally for six months—by using your savings and other resources?	___	___
Do you owe the government for any debts?	___	___
Do you have any long-standing legal problems?	___	___
Is there some other personal or professional problem that you know you need to begin working on today?	___	___

If you answered "Yes" to any question, then the time to start working on your transition is right now.

What needs to be done should be obvious. In most cases, on-base resources can help. Squeamishness about letting anyone in a uniform know about your trouble with alcohol, a financial difficulty, a legal entanglement, or chronic health problem doesn't make sense anymore.

If you're nearing your separation date, don't worry about how things will look on your military record. The only personal problems that call for discretion are the ones that might prevent you from getting an honorable discharge. For the rest, make use of the free resources the military has provided.

Action to Take: _____

Date _____

Person to See _____

Address _____

_____

_____

Phone _____

Action to Take: _____

Date _____

Person to See _____

Address _____

_____

_____

Phone _____

Action to Take: _____

Date _____

Person to See _____

Address _____

_____

_____

Phone _____

Other Tasks _____

_____

_____

2

Beginnings and Endings: Seven Truths for a Successful Transition

Changes are difficult. Going from the military to the civilian world is one of the most difficult changes of all. In fact, it's not a single change, but a bucketful of changes.

Everyone leaving the military changes jobs, but many veterans will find themselves in an unfamiliar corner of their old career field, or perhaps in an entirely different line of work. Homes and friends change. Most importantly, there's a fundamental shift in who you are, what you do that's valued by society, and where you fit into the world.

"It's not just a job," the recruiting slogans have proclaimed for years, and they've been right. But it's also more than an adventure. To be on active duty is to be connected in a mysterious way to people and events that extend from George Washington at Valley Forge to Norman Schwarzkopf in Desert Storm. Breaking your links to the military is painful. Forging new bonds to

*During each day since the end of
World War II, nearly 500 people
have left active duty.*

the civilian world—from finding a new job to settling into a new home—is difficult and time-consuming.

But there's another dimension of the military that can help during this confusing, stressful time. The services have a treasury of wisdom, helpful tips, and money-saving resources for the person facing a return to the civilian world, a treasury built up over generations and founded on the simple fact that everyone in the U.S. military, from Washington to Schwarzkopf, has had to take off the uniform at some point.

This may be the first transition for you or for your spouse, but there's a wealth of information available on how to make that change, drawn from the experiences of people who've already walked out of the main gate for the last time.

Before looking at the finer points of leaving the military and finding a meaningful place in the private sector, let's start with a broad view and examine the seven truths for a successful transition:

Successful Transitions Begin Early
Many federal benefits geared toward assisting military personnel and their families through their transitions don't begin until people are within 180 days of leaving active duty.

That doesn't mean the 180-day mark is when you should begin preparing yourself for a return to the civilian work force. The sooner the better, whether the question is getting discretionary medical or dental treatment, learning about veterans' benefits, or even trying your hand at writing a resume. The more you do now, the less will be left for those last, frantic months in uniform.

In fact, beginning with the first day you spend on active duty you should keep an eye on your personal D-Day, or Discharge Day. It will arrive, and the more advance preparation you make, the easier it will be.

By talking to people and reading while on active duty, you can refine your understanding of veterans' programs, the employment needs of the private sector, and the marketability of your military skills.

Perhaps you can make a minor change in your military career—such as getting a certain assignment or attending a professional education course—that would have small meaning to the military, but a large payback on your resume.

Or you could take classes at night or during weekends. Despite the value of military training and on-the-job experiences, the best preparation for the civilian work force is still civilian education. Each installation has an education office with full details on courses available locally and the rules for getting Uncle Sam to pick up the tab.

If there's nothing you're interested in studying or if you're not sure what you'd like to do "on the outside," the education office has free aptitude tests for military personnel. Those tests can help you identify what you do best.

You can't get too much education. The government programs that help military people further their civilian educations are a national treasure. They are rarely matched by anything in the private sector. Take advantage of as many as you can, and start early in your military career.

Successful Transitions Are Self-Aware

One veteran was unemployed for months. Some days, the discouragement was more than he could bear. During the worst times, instead of fighting his fears, he'd let them expand to their logical conclusion.

He'd imagine his neighbors opening their morning newspapers one day and learning about his family's problems in a story that carried this headline:

STARVED VETERAN FOUND IN $150,000 HOME—EMACIATED FAMILY HUDDLED AROUND BASEMENT TV

The imaginary headline let the veteran put his troubles into perspective. That's not a headline anyone actually sees. Even the longest transition ends, and the folks with the least marketable skills find a productive niche in the civilian work force.

Active-duty job seekers need to be aware of the pressures they are under, and they need to deal with their fears and frustrations, both during their final months in uniform and their first months as civilians. At a minimum, they need to:

- Spend at least an hour a week dropping all "brave fronts" and talking about feelings to a friend, spouse, parent, or counselor. Men, this means you.
- Avoid dwelling on the negatives. "Contingency planning" is a useful military technique, but it shouldn't be confused with "awfulizing," or letting yourself concentrate on how awful everything is and how much worse it's going to become.
- Give yourself short breaks during the day, and longer breaks a couple times a week, to do things that are fun and diverting.
- Pay attention to physical activity. Transition is a time to increase, rather than decrease, your exercise.
- Watch your alcohol consumption. There isn't a single one of life's problems that can't be worsened by a generous application of liquor.

Successful Transitions Are Paced
"Getting a job *is* a job," someone once observed. And every job seeker who has heard that phrase has been exposed to a major

> *Will your job search be a sprint or marathon? Can you sustain your pace if it ends up being a marathon?*

truth. To find well-paying, meaningful work takes a major investment of time, effort, and creativity.

Like many truths, this has been corrupted. "Getting a job is *more* than a job," one version asserts. "You gotta spend at least 60 hours a week at it."

Others contend that anyone who puts only 60 hours a week into the job search probably wants to be unemployed. The seven-day-a-week search is the only true schedule for a sincere job hunter, according to others.

There are real dangers in these exaggerated claims of how much time and effort you should spend looking for a job. Partly, it's the risk of getting an interview and showing up haggard and fuzzy-brained. Partly, it's the risk of constantly scrambling so hard that you don't take the time to figure out what you really want and how to get it.

The greatest danger, however, befalls those who end up with a lengthy stretch of unemployment after leaving the military. They don't need to manufacture reasons to feel bad. But many of them do exactly that, as they torture themselves with fantasies about how smoothly the search would have gone if they'd only spent 80 hours a week doing it.

What's a reasonable pace? Many people start out at a sprint, then throttle back. They will put more time into the search again when financial pressures increase.

The best rule is to plan—physically, emotionally, financially—for a marathon.

That planning starts while you're still in uniform. As you attend to the details of leaving active duty, adopt a pace that you can sustain for the long haul. Don't let yourself become physically exhausted and emotionally wrung out before you even receive your discharge papers. You might not be in shape either to look for work or to handle the demands of a new job.

Successful Transitions Are Marked by a Constant Search for Tools

One kind of person shows up with distressing regularity at the offices of the counselors who help active-duty folks find jobs in the civilian work force. This person is dejected, unemployed, with dwindling savings, eager as much for emotional support as practical assistance.

These are the former believers in the Three-Step Transition. They had left the military weeks, even months, before, shaking their heads at the poor chumps who had to waste their time with job counselors, transition seminars, and resume-writing books. Practitioners of the Three-Step Transition don't need such hand-holding foolishness, because they are "a leader among leaders, and a manager among managers."

What is a Three-Step Transition?
- Step One: Let the civilian world know you're available.
- Step Two: Try not to get crushed by the stampede of people rushing to your door as you sort through the offers.
- Step Three: Accept the best offer, but even then, be tough in negotiating the details. Everyone knows how woefully underpaid the military is. You shouldn't settle for a civilian job unless it pays two, three, even four times more than your active-duty paycheck.

The Three-Step Transition is a wonderful, natural fantasy, but it's only a fantasy. Anyone who acts upon it is likely to face a bitter period of rejection and unemployment.

By contrast, another veteran going through transition described himself as "an information vacuum," drawing in all the data he could find about looking for work, writing resumes, conducting himself at interviews, and obtaining his full federal benefits. After a while, information becomes redundant. But the successful job seeker is constantly searching for any nugget that will be useful.

Yes, you may already know 90 percent of the information presented in the three-day class of the Transition Assistance Program. But in the 10 percent you don't know may be the one piece of information that will make a difference in ending your own unemployment.

Successful Transitions Are Focused on Skills

The training and on-the-job experiences offered during a typical tour in uniform are valued by managers in the private sector. A veteran with an honorable discharge is a proven worker, disciplined, drug-free, acquainted with stress and the ways of the workplace.

The military isn't shy about telling active-duty people how much better they are than their civilian counterparts. From the first day at basic training, new recruits receive a thousand messages—both subtle and blatant—about how their experiences in uniform will eventually be rewarded when they return to the civilian job market.

"I've been trained to lead people in combat," is the message many veterans give hiring supervisors. "If the United States military says I can do that, then there's nothing your nine-to-five job can throw at me that I can't handle."

Unfortunately, it isn't that easy. Except for entry-level positions, each civilian job requires specific skills and direct working experiences. Self-confidence and broad assertions about the quality of military training lead to few quality paychecks in the private sector.

"Overqualified" can mean "unfocused."
What skills are you trying to sell?
Will you accept a job that pays you
solely for using those skills?

To be successful, veterans have to convince a civilian supervisor that they have the exact skills and experiences needed to fill a specific vacancy.

Job-hunting veterans must focus on each vacancy, gathering as much information as possible about the job, the company, even the supervisor. Then they must show through applications, resumes, letters, interviews, references, and networking that they're the ideal candidate for the position.

Job seekers are trying to hit a target. And it doesn't matter whether they fall short, land wide, or over-shoot. A miss is a miss.

The target is a specific vacancy, and the successful job seekers are the ones who demonstrate to hiring supervisors that their skills directly match the ones needed for the job at hand. No more, and no less.

Successful Transitions Are Demilitarized
The morale of one new retiree was painfully low after the first twenty resumes produced rejection letters and unreturned telephone calls.

What was wrong with these civilians, he wondered. He was young, he was willing to get his hands dirty, he would put in long hours. It didn't take a leap of faith for these civilians to see what he could do. For he had laid it all out in his resume. He had been a great lieutenant colonel.

And then it struck him. He hadn't been applying for his first civilian job. Instead, he had been justifying his last military one. "Without thinking about it, I had tailored that resume to show I was the best person available in the entire world to fill my old active-duty job," he said.

This veteran learned a great truth. Being a veteran won't get you a job. Military titles don't get jobs. Medals don't get jobs. Even work histories don't get jobs. Skills get jobs.

Supervisors hire the people who most clearly possess the skills necessary to get a job done. Too many veterans devise elaborate resumes that show how much responsibility they had shouldered while on active duty. If they possess the skills the civilian supervisor is looking for, that information is often buried under a clutter of titles, acronyms, decorations, and (to the civilian) irrelevant accomplishments.

If you want a good job, you must convince a civilian supervisor that you have the necessary skills. The odds are that you won't be able to do that if you're unconsciously applying for the last job you held in uniform.

Successful Transitions Evolve

Self-confidence is one of the hallmarks of a successful tour on active duty. It's also a vital survival tool for everyone who struggles from bed in the morning to face the rejections, disappointments, and doubts that are part of setting a career onto a new path.

But self-confidence shouldn't be confused with pig-headedness. Few people leaving active duty have ever done it before. Most have never looked for full-time work in the private sector. So, part of a successful transition involves leaving a few chinks open in the armor of your self-confidence to learn.

As some of the personal stories earlier in this chapter suggest, veterans have to be open to feedback. They must be flexible in their approach to finding a job in the civilian work force. Not

---

*Each transition is a journey. You
can't cover much ground if your
ideas, attitudes, knowledge, and
skills stay in one place.*

---

all advice is equally effective in all career fields and communities,
and not every veteran is skillful with each job-hunting tool.

Good jobs are the ones in which you know your strengths and
interests and channel your efforts in that direction. In the same
way, getting to that job requires a personalized approach that
capitalizes on your strengths, lets you stay keenly attuned to signs
of what works, and maintains your ability to adjust when situations and your job-hunting skills change.

3

Morale Check

"Transition" is a neat word, an antiseptic word, a misleading word. Lurking behind those three syllables are enough decisions to choke an efficiency expert and enough hassles to make any sensible psychologist wonder if substance abuse might not have its positive aspects.

Under the best of circumstances, your emotional, mental, and physical resources will be taxed to the limit by the pressures of settling into a new home, a new job, a new life.

If your return to the civilian world is normal—that is, if it's riddled with uncertainties and risks—you can probably elevate your blood pressure 10 or 15 points just by thinking about packing crates and resumes.

Ask yourself a few simple questions:

- Have you adopted an attitude and a schedule for your transition efforts that you can sustain?
- If you keep doing for months what you're doing today, will your mind be clear, your body rested, and your spirits up?

- Do you believe that you're entitled to have a life now, that life isn't something that's "on hold" until after the current unpleasantness has been resolved?

Have any of these questions made you squirm? It's time for a morale check.

THE BIG "B"—BOOZE

	Yes	No
Have you been drinking more alcohol, or drinking more frequently, since you began transition planning?	___	___
Have you been drunk during the last three months?	___	___
Have you failed to perform some actions for your transition because you were drunk or hung over?	___	___
Have you been arrested or been in trouble at work for situations aggravated by drinking or hangovers?	___	___
Do you believe you wouldn't drink so much if you didn't have all your current problems?	___	___
Are you uncomfortable with the amount or frequency of your drinking?	___	___

If you answered "Yes" to any question, you should consider talking to a professional about your drinking and your transition efforts. That's not to say you're an alcoholic, or even a problem drinker. But something isn't right. You are not handling the transition properly, or the transition is forcing other problems to the forefront. Make an appointment *today* with a chaplain, physician, or counselor:

Appointment Date _____

Person to See _____

Address _____

_____

Phone _____

If you answered "Yes" to two questions, you should seriously consider attending a meeting of Alcoholics Anonymous. Again, you may not be an alcoholic, or even a problem drinker. But for you, drinking is getting in the way of living. Check your local telephone book *today* for the number for Alcoholics Anonymous. Call and ask for the date, time, and place of the next meeting. Show up and listen. See what they've got that you can use.

Meeting Date _____

Meeting Time _____

Address _____

_____

If you answered "Yes" to three or more questions, you've probably already wondered if booze is getting the better of you. It's starting to look that way. You need more than a quick look-see at an A.A. meeting. You need to talk personally to folks who've already faced their own problems with the bottle.

Check the local telephone book *today* for the A.A. number, then call for the date, time, and place of the next A.A. meeting. After the meeting get the telephone numbers of three people who talked during the meeting and who seemed to make sense to you. *(Yes, that means walking up to perfect strangers and asking them to help you. But give it a try. Their reactions will surprise you.)* Then call each one during the next week.

Person _____

Phone _____

Date to Call _____

Person _____

Phone _____

Date to Call _____

Person _____

Phone _____

Date to Call _____

YOU'VE GOT A BODY, TOO

	Yes	*No*
Do you get your heart rate up for 20 minutes at least three times a week? (No, sex doesn't count.)	___	___
Do you break into a sweat at least three times a week? (It still doesn't count.)	___	___
Do you do something physical at least once a week that's fun? (Talk about one-track minds!) Something like racquetball or tennis?	___	___

A regular exercise program should be part of your transition training. It clears the mind, relaxes the body, improves the immune system, and makes you feel better. It's not a luxury you can resume after life settles down.

Leaving the military, finding a civilian job, moving to a new home, and recreating life's routines are endurance tests. Exercise is one of nature's ways to build up endurance.

If you're not already exercising for at least 20 minutes on three days every week, then make exercise part of your schedule. Don't leave it to chance. Don't worry whether there are more productive things to do. Just do it.

Weekly Exercise

Day 1 _____

   Time _____

   Event _____

Day 2 _____

   Time _____

   Event _____

Day 3 _____

   Time _____

   Event _____

Weekend Special

   Day _____

   Time _____

   Event _____

DURING THE LAST WEEK . . .

	Yes	*No*
Have you seen a movie—in a theater, on TV, or on the VCR?	____	____

	Yes	*No*
Did you have at least 30 minutes to read a book or some interesting stories from a magazine or newspaper?	——	——
Have you laughed out loud?	——	——
Have you had at least one conversation in which you could let down your guard?	——	——
Has someone told you something that made you feel touched that they trusted you?	——	——
Have you talked with an elderly person?	——	——
Have you held a child?	——	——
Have you petted a dog or cat?	——	——
Have you noticed something in nature and thought, "That's pretty"?	——	——
Have you complimented at least one person every day?	——	——
Okay, okay. Have you had sex?	——	——

There are no right or wrong answers to these questions. There's only life. And these simple activities are pieces of a complete and satisfying life. Life doesn't stop while you're leaving active duty. You shouldn't allow yourself to miss any of it.

What are you going to start doing today to get a life? Put it in writing. Make a promise to yourself.

"I promise to put some life into my transition by":

_____

_____

4

Who Goes, Who Stays?

You will decide how to handle your own transition back to the
private sector. Unfortunately, you may have little say in deciding
when to leave.

Since the troops who won the American Revolution were
demobilized after the final battle at Yorktown more than 200
years ago, a U.S. victory has always resulted in soldiers, sailors,
and Marines madly scrambling back to the civilian world, leaving
an active-duty force that was depleted of experienced manpower
and tragically vulnerable to the next aggressor who swaggered
onto the world stage.

The post–Cold War drawdown is a historic oddity. For once,
the threat to the nation's security has been eliminated, but the
troops don't want to go home. The present drawdown is the first
one concerned with nudging folks toward the door instead of
being worried about holding onto them.

Still, the Pentagon's manpower planners are harkening to the
lessons of the past. They don't want to plant seeds today that will
result in a feeble, stunted force in the future, one unable to

---

*Can you leave the military with six
months' notice and no separation
pay or exit bonus? If you can, you're
in good shape. That's the worst-case
transition scenario.*

---

withstand the ravages of the next storm that sweeps over the
international community.

The manpower planners are determined to ensure that both
during the drawdown and after it's over, the U.S. military keeps
people in the right skills and with the proper levels of experience
to preserve an active-duty force that can respond to any military
challenges.

In this chapter, we will look at various rules and programs
used by the military to decide the most basic questions of who
goes and who is permitted to stay in uniform.

THE "TWO BY FOURS" OF THE DRAWDOWN

It's one of the ironies of the modern military that capable people
who want to stay in uniform are being forced out, while other
active-duty folks who would prefer to resume their civilian careers
are denied the chance to leave.

Credit that irony to the two "by's" that govern the decisions
of personnel experts as to who will go and who will stay. When
military personnel are considered for discharge, they are lumped
together:

- By military skill;
- And by rank.

In other words, manpower planners want to ensure that they keep
enough people in each skill and career field to do the necessary

jobs, and within those overall numbers, the military wants to retain the right distribution of folks throughout the rank structure.

Those two "by's" are multiplied by four. That's the four services—Army, Navy, Air Force, and Marine Corps. Each service makes its own decisions about the number of people in each skill and in each rank to retain or separate. The fifth service, the Coast Guard, which in peacetime takes on law-enforcement duties under the U.S. Department of Transportation, probably will avoid any personnel cutbacks during the 1990s.

Thus, to know the retention or discharge chances for any individual, it's necessary to know that person's:

• Branch of service;
• Skill or career field;
• And rank.

The system can result in apparent inequities. An E-5 who specializes in microwave communications for the Army may be highly vulnerable to an involuntary discharge, for example. Meanwhile, an E-6 microwave specialist in the Army may face a secure career, as may an E-5 microwave specialist in the Navy or Air Force.

EARLY-OUT PROGRAMS

Despite the Hollywood stereotype that depicts senior military people as being not very bright, even the Pentagon's leadership can figure out that the easiest, fastest, cheapest way to reduce the active-duty force is to give discharge papers to the people who want to leave.

Called "early outs," these programs allow enlisted people nearing the end of their enlistments, plus officers approaching the end of their obligated time on active duty, to return to the civilian world a little sooner than expected.

Usually the time shaved off the active-duty commitment is

Did the military pay for your civilian education? The price of an early-out may include repayment.

measured in days and weeks. Occasionally it can amount to three months. Longer periods are rare.

As with so many drawdown programs, the military will take volunteers for early outs, but first manpower officials will set guidelines on who will be allowed to volunteer. Those scheduled to be discharged between certain official, published dates are the only ones eligible to apply for those early outs.

Eligibility may depend on another factor. In keeping with the general shape of other drawdown programs, the early-out window may be opened only for people by rank or by career field.

Will you be offered an early out? There are few certainties about when a new early-out window will open, or when an existing one will close. The best you can hope to get is a rough estimate about the likelihood. Consider two questions:

- If your discharge were scheduled for next month, would your service let you apply for an early out?
- If your discharge were scheduled a year ago, would your service have let you apply for an early out? That is, if you're scheduled for discharge on October 1993, would you have qualified for an early out on October 1992?

If you can answer "Yes" to both, or "No" to both, then you can see the general direction that recent trends have followed.

Flexibility is the watchword for everyone planning for a successful transition. There are no guarantees that long-standing programs for early outs will continue.

Are you an effective consumer of information on transition policies? Do you read Army Times, Navy Times, Air Force Times, *and the publications of veterans groups and the military?*

MORE ON EARLY OUTS

You may not have to worry about fitting through the legal hoops that surround the early-out programs created for the drawdown. You may be able to design your own hoops. Military regulations have provisions—completely unrelated to the overall cutback in the size of the uniformed force—that allow an early release from active duty for some people. These early outs are approved on a case-by-case basis, usually for educational reasons or for family hardships. Here are some more details.

Education

If some people are released from active duty a few weeks early, they can begin immediately attending civilian classes. By contrast, if the military held them to their normal discharge date, they would have to wait four to six months for the next semester to begin.

If you are in a situation like that, you may qualify for an educational early out. Normally, it reduces your time in uniform by less than 90 days. In extraordinary circumstances—such as being accepted by a medical school or being offered a one-time scholarship—the military can shave 180 days from your commitment.

Educational early outs are based on informal, subjective decisions. There are few guidelines. There are, however, a few things to keep in mind:

- Usually, you won't be considered for an early out unless you've already been accepted by a school.
- You may deserve an early out, but you won't get it if the military needs people in your career field.
- This program exists to help people in unusual circumstances. Don't clog up the system with frivolous applications.

Hardships

A change in family circumstances can put incredible pressures upon a service member. Sometimes, the best thing for the person in uniform, for the family, and even for the military is to release someone from active duty to take care of these responsibilities.

The military's senior leadership has broad authority to grant early outs based upon family hardships. The guidelines for handling hardship cases are even looser than for educational early outs. There are no limits on the amount of time that can be forgiven.

Typically, hardship early outs are approved for illnesses in the family that require the service member's care or the service member's help running a family-owned business.

Approval isn't automatic, even when family members are gravely ill or a family business is on the verge of bankruptcy. The presence of the military member must be indispensable for dealing with the emergency.

Sometimes the problems that can be solved by a hardship early out can also be solved by other means, principally a so-called compassionate reassignment. That's a transfer that moves—or keeps—an active-duty member near the home of a relative with special medical needs.

The phrase "early out" can be misleading in this instance.

Usually, an early out is sought near the end of an obligated time in uniform, something that will trim a few weeks or months from active-duty time.

Many circumstances that justify a hardship early out will also justify a discharge at any time, regardless of how far people are from the end of their commitments to the military.

Even more than with educational early outs, the philosophy that says "It doesn't hurt to try," has no place here.

Hardship early outs have been established to help military people confronting painful family emergencies, usually situations involving the imminent death of a loved one. Frivolous applications make it more difficult for the people who urgently need help.

CUTTING SHORT MILITARY CAREERS

The majority of people who leave active duty share one common characteristic. They are taking off their uniforms because they're at the end of their commitments to the military. Their enlistments have expired or, if they're officers, they've fulfilled their initial obligated terms of service.

But the normal flow of people back to the civilian world isn't large enough or fast enough to shrink the active-duty force to the manpower goals set for the drawdown. A number of procedures—some quite traditional within the military and others newly invented for the current drawdown—have been set up to hasten the return of people to the private sector.

Denied Reenlistment, Denial of Continuation
When a service has too many people wearing the same rank or serving in the same career field—or, most typically, wearing the same rank within one career field—there's an easy, obvious way to control the total number of people in uniform.

Some situations that lead to denied reenlistments will also prevent enlisted members from being promoted or given extra training or education.

When the time comes for enlisted members to reenlist, they're not allowed to sign on for another hitch. This is called a "denied reenlistment." For officers, the equivalent is called "being denied continuation."

Being denied reenlistment or being denied continuance isn't a reflection upon a military person's ability or contribution to the country. It's strictly a way for the personnel commands to ensure a steady, orderly reduction of the active-duty population.

People with careers cut short by these administrative mechanisms are generally eligible for the full range of veterans' benefits. The main criterion for most veterans' benefits is a discharge that is rated as honorable or general.

They may also be eligible for separation pay, which is a special one-time bonus that is a sort of financial recognition for the hardships and inconveniences of having a career and home life disrupted.

Often, however, denial of reenlistment occurs because enlisted members have failed to meet some expectation or standard. These are called "reenlistment bars."

That failure isn't serious enough to warrant an immediate discharge, but it is enough to justify a termination of the enlisted member's military career at the next convenient milestone, which in most cases is the time of reenlistment.

Reenlistment bars may be imposed when someone refuses to accept an overseas assignment. People in an over-strength skill

---

*VSI and SSB can't go to first-
termers or military retirees.*

---

may encounter a bar if they decline the chance to retrain into
an under-strength skill.

Exit Bonuses

Since December 1991, the Defense Department has had the
authority to offer special financial incentives to persuade service
members to leave active duty voluntarily.

They are called the Voluntary Separation Incentive (VSI) and
Special Separation Benefit (SSB). A third kind of financial payment going to discharged service members—Separation Pay—
isn't classified as an exit bonus, since it goes to people whose
departure from active duty is involuntary.

Despite being part of the voluntary discharge process, VSI and
SSB don't go to everyone who requests them. Each service defines
categories of people—usually by rank and by career field—who
are eligible to apply.

Usually, each service's personnel command announces the
ranks and career fields eligible to apply. Eligibility can also be
limited by other factors. For example, to volunteer for VSI or
SSB, a service member might have to be stationed in the United
States, or not owe the government time on active duty because
of government-paid civilian education, or be tapped for involuntary separation under some other personnel procedure.

Whenever VSI and SSB are opened for volunteers, the official
announcements specify deadlines for applications, and sometimes
deadlines for actually leaving active duty. Applications are sub-
mitted through the unit personnel office.

If enough volunteers aren't received by the deadline, the personnel commands can reopen the search for volunteers. There aren't any guarantees that will happen, however.

Once service members are accepted for an exit bonus, they can choose either VSI or SSB. The government cannot restrict their choice to either of the two bonuses.

High-Year of Tenure, Promotion Boards

"Up or Out" has long been the rule in the military's personnel system. Active-duty people are expected to head up the promotion ladder at a minimal rate. Those who don't keep up the pace find themselves civilians again.

For the enlisted force, the key phrase is "High-Year of Tenure." It's expressed in terms of years on active duty per rank. For example, the High-Year of Tenure point for an E-6 may be 20 years. If someone is still an E-6 after 20 years on active duty, then he or she has to retire.

Officers have a more complicated system. Promotion boards look at the records of officers within certain ranks and career fields. The boards decide either to promote an officer, or they "pass over"—or, put another way, they decline to recommend— an officer for promotion.

Officers in the grade of O-1 or O-2 who have been passed over once for promotion are vulnerable to receive an involuntary discharge.

An officer in the grade of O-3 or O-4 who has been twice "passed over" is vulnerable to receive an involuntary discharge.

Officers in the grade of O-5 or higher aren't vulnerable, necessarily, to discharge after two pass overs, but they could be forced to take early retirements, as explained in the section below on SERBs.

Among the legal shadings in a promotion board's decisions:
• Officers rated as "fully qualified" are basically in an over-

crowded career field. They are eligible to receive separation pay.

- Officers rated as "not fully qualified" are denied promotion because of some professional shortcoming. They may receive half the regular separation pay, or they may be denied separation pay entirely.

As with so much fine print in the personnel regulations, each service does things differently. During the drawdown, military people should anticipate changes in the rules on High-Year of Tenure and promotion boards.

SERBs

Other techniques that the personnel commands are relying upon during the drawdown involve taking a look at people who already qualify for full military retirement benefits. If selected, retirement-eligible people are forced to hang up their uniforms earlier than planned.

For officers—and in some services, for enlisted people, too— the process is called "Selective Early Retirement Boards" (SERBs). These are formal administrative evaluations of someone's military career and projected usefulness to the government.

A formal exchange of paperwork surrounds the SERBs. Everyone whose personnel file goes before one of the boards is notified in advance and given the chance to review the records and submit additional information.

The results of a SERB are in writing, and personnel have formal rights of appeal.

Until 1991, SERBs were strictly a worry for officers. Since then, however, individual services have begun using a version of SERBs for the enlisted ranks. Usually, the focus remains on the top three enlisted ranks.

Generally, military members must have at least 20 years on active duty—and, therefore, eligibility to retirement benefits—

before being reviewed by a SERB. Officers with 18 years can also have their records go before a panel, but if selected they will be allowed to spend two more years on active duty to earn retired pay.

Everyone picked by a SERB board is ordered to retire. They receive the same benefits as everyone who volunteers for retirement.

VOLUNTARY VERSUS INVOLUNTARY DISCHARGES

The hottest debate in most barracks, berthing areas, and military dormitories these days involves the finer points of deciding what kind of discharge qualifies a military person for being "involuntarily separated," in comparison with the discharge that meets the official definition of a "voluntary separation."

It's more than an academic debate. A lot of money hangs on the answer. Congress and the Pentagon have created many benefits, bonuses, and programs to soften the blows that hit people who leave active duty.

The largest number of benefits go to the people who have "voluntary separation"—or the equivalent—stamped on their discharge papers. Service members who accept certain voluntary discharges qualify for bonuses in the tens of thousands, even the hundreds of thousands, of dollars.

So, why do usually knowledgeable people with years in uniform disagree about what fits the "voluntary separation" definition? Surely, it's a matter of looking it up in the regulations?

It's not that easy. Understanding why it's not easy is necessary to avoid the legal web that we call "The *Voluntary Separation* Trap."

Many people, from first-termers to careerists, have already fallen victim to this trap. Ironically, the ones who tried hardest to avoid it are most likely to become ensnared.

They are the people who spent hours combing through federal laws in the base library. They put in additional hours hunting through the regulations. All this work was to make sure that their discharge would fit the official requirements for being voluntary.

Armed with the certainty of that research, they made plans for returning to the civilian world . . . only to find out during their last hours in uniform that the military doesn't consider their discharges to be voluntary.

Or perhaps the discharge is voluntary, but no benefits are attached to their kind of voluntary separation. The benefits and the bonuses these people got were a miserly fraction of what they had planned to receive.

Understanding what happened to them will help others avoid "The *Voluntary Separation* Trap." Here are the major lessons.

There's No Single Definition of "Voluntary Separation"

Every time Congress has passed a law changing the benefits for people leaving active duty against their will, lawmakers have used a slightly different definition of "voluntary separation." The Pentagon has done the same when writing its regulations.

Some barracks lawyers have been burned. Or they hurt friends. They ran across a definition of "voluntary separation" in the law books or the regulations, and they assumed they had found the one, absolute definition that fits all cases.

It didn't. That definition doesn't exist.

No One Fits into One Definition Very Long

The military's personnel machine constantly moves people at its own pace, and for its own reasons, from one legalistic category to another.

Someone who turns down the chance to accept a voluntary discharge this year could be handed an involuntary discharge next year. No one can expect a second chance to accept a voluntary discharge.

Fitting into the Right Definition Doesn't Mean You'll Get the Benefit

Many important transition benefits aren't rock-solid legal rights. Military commanders sometimes have discretion in deciding who gets what.

This applies especially to non-monetary benefits like living in government quarters after discharge, getting time off from work to attend seminars or to look for work, or getting government-paid travel for a spouse.

Generally, commanders don't have any latitude in deciding who gets the major benefits like the exit bonuses, medical coverage, and the GI Bill.

Fitting into the Right Definition and Screwing Up Means You Won't Get Anything

Separation pay has been around a long time, and it has gone to people who leave the military involuntarily. But it's not a right owed to all the people who leave active duty against their will.

Plenty of departures are arranged every year, over protest, for folks who've made so much trouble and performed so poorly that the military doesn't want them anymore.

This is not the class of people Congress wanted to help when it passed laws setting up the various transition benefits.

There are loopholes in many programs that allow military officials to deny benefits to people with bad records, even if they otherwise pass through most of the legal hoops that lead to special transition help.

Generally, no special benefits go to people receiving discharges that are rated as dishonorable, bad conduct, or under other than honorable conditions.

Not All the Definitions Make Sense
There are plenty of military people with perfectly honorable records who want to stay in uniform, who are leaving against their wills, but who are officially rated as receiving voluntary separations.

Remember this is a region governed by fine print in laws and regulations, not the subtleties of human motivations or even common sense.

Consider the case of the careerist forced into retirement, the first-termer denied a chance to sign up for a second hitch, or the mid-career person who sees the axe coming and decides to quit before it lands.

In these three cases, there's nothing voluntary about the person's departure from active duty. But, generally, the service member in each of these examples doesn't officially qualify as an involuntary separation.

The Definitions Don't Often Matter
The reason there's a package of transition benefits is that Congress and the Pentagon want to help military people adjust to civilian life.

Lawmakers and Pentagon officials were eager to put most assistance within reach of the largest number of people, not to split legal hairs about who's qualified for what.

Consequently, many of the programs that military people think of as helping only the people who receive the exit bonuses for voluntary discharges are actually available to everyone leaving active duty.

Government-sponsored job-training seminars, personal counseling, access to computerized job banks, the use of selected computers and printers to make resumes—these are some of the resources that everyone can use.

In fact, the doors to some of these basic benefits have been opened so widely that they're also available to reservists, spouses, and federal civilians.

To Get Direct Information, Ask Direct Questions

Any sentence that begins, "If I'm involuntarily discharged, will I get . . ." is doomed to continue the misunderstandings. It's no better to ask, "If I'm voluntarily discharged, will I get . . ."

A clear appreciation of individual benefits comes from a sentence that begins simply: "When I'm discharged, will I get . . ."

That question, asked of a knowledgeable commander, career counselor, or transition official, will likely be answered by a series of questions to determine the specific circumstances surrounding a discharge.

Only then, armed with the facts about an individual service member, can an expert really answer the questions expertly.

5

Five-Step Financial Self-Analysis

A successful transition involves taking action long before you have to take action. By the same standard, by getting your financial house in order as soon as possible, you'll be spared the worry and effort of dealing with all your aggravations—new job, new home, perhaps new career, and often a new level of income—at the same time.

Like many transition actions, there are things you can do financially months in advance of your discharge date. But before you can figure out where your family's spending-level needs to go, you must get a clear picture of where you are today.

You need, in a word, a budget.

Household budgets are like household first-aid kits. Everyone knows a responsible homeowner should have one, but not every household follows through. Too often it seems that budgets are for people with real money.

Your money, your debts, and your dreams for your financial future are real enough. Getting a grip on your cash-flow can be done in less time than it takes to watch a movie.

After doing a budget, many people are stunned to find out that things aren't as bad as they feared. And they're amazed to realize how much control they can wrest over their own spending. Give it a try. You have nothing to lose but your powerlessness.

Step One
Get a pocket calculator, a few sheets of paper, and your financial records for the past six months. This includes your checkbook, credit card statements, bank statements, and any other financial record or receipt.
- Write down everything you spent money on during the past six months.
- Put a one- or two-word description—like "Rent" or "Birthday gifts"—next to each amount.
- How much cash did you spend? Did you use cash for any major purchases? Write that down, too.
- Add up your expenses for each month.
- Add up the six monthly totals, then divide by six.

This gives you a reasonable monthly average for your expenses.

Step Two
Make a list of any monthly expenses you won't have after discharge.

Are there any realistic belt-tightening measures you can make? (Planning to live on chicken soup and unbuttered bread isn't realistic.)

Are there any major bills you can pay off before your discharge?

Step Three
Adjust your monthly average for expenses by some of the reasonable economies you discovered in Step Two.

Step Four
Add together your assets, including checking accounts, savings accounts, and money that you'll receive for exit bonuses.

Don't include Individual Retirement Accounts. Remember that you may be eligible for unemployment compensation, with adjustments for any exit bonuses.

In light of the adjusted monthly average for expenses that you developed in Step Three, how long can you pay the bills after your discharge if you're unemployed?

Step Five
Take a long look at your figures. Should you be getting an extra job now? Would prolonged unemployment be disastrous? Are any real danger signs there? Here are some things to look for:

	Yes	No
During the last six months, did you have to use a credit card to pay for normal living expenses?	___	___
Do you owe the government money for delinquent taxes or other debts?	___	___
Can you pay your bills for at least two months— and ideally for six months—if you are unemployed?	___	___
Are you comfortable and realistic about your financial situation after D-Day?	___	___

If you answered "Yes" to either of the first two questions, or "No" to either of the two last two questions, then make an appointment *today* to get free help with financial planning from your on-base community service center, family support center, or family service center:

Appointment Date _____

Person to See _____

Address _____

_____

_____

Phone _____

Notes _____

_____

_____

_____

_____

_____

_____

_____

6

Getting Back to Work:
The Networking Connection

If you've decided to leave active duty—or if the government has decided for you—then you must make some decisions about the general shape that your post-military life will take. Time, effort, and more information are often necessary to decide.

Where will you live?

Most veterans return to their hometowns, but many strike off in new directions. Even when the choice is based on "gut feelings" or family ties, it's important to make sure that you understand the local cost of living and employment picture. Libraries and transition offices can point you toward the right data.

What will you do?

A surprisingly large proportion of new veterans aren't sure. Some came on active duty because there weren't any clear choices in the civilian sector. Others learned a trade in the military only to discover they didn't want to spend the rest of their working lives doing it. Whatever the reason, this is a common story, nothing that should cause embarrassment. Luckily, each major installation has an education office where free aptitude tests are available. The tests won't tell you what to do, but they're proven winners in making people think about their skills and interests in new ways.

Who will you work for?

Ah, there's the rub. Of all the decisions facing a newly discharged veteran, it's the one most directly tied to your economic survival and the one over which you have the least control. While you may decide that you'd like to work for someone, that person will decide whether you'll be allowed to work for him or her.

Fortunately, there's no shortage of books, articles, news programs, seminars, classes, even videotapes on how to get a job. Much of the information applies to military people coming off active duty as well as to civilians. Local transition offices can make recommendations about the best. Keep in mind that one book or class isn't going to tell you all you need to know. You must scoop up useful information wherever you find it. Until you're established again in the civilian work force, learning about jobs and job hunting should be part of your daily routine.

Perhaps because of the flood of how-to information available to job seekers, it's easy for your eye to drift off the target.

Let's look at the process of finding employment in reverse, starting with the action that signals your search is at an end. That's when someone reaches a hand across a desk, flashes a big smile and says, "I really want you to join my team. As far as I'm concerned, you're hired."

If that's the last thing that happens before your job search ends, then what's the next to the last thing that happens?

Obviously, it's the conversation you had with the person who had hiring authority. That's what will take you, directly and immediately, into the ranks of the employed.

> *The successful resume only leads to*
> *a job interview.*
> *The successful job interview leads*
> *to a job.*

While battling through a hurricane of unpleasant emotions, struggling to master the intricacies of the job search, and wrenching loose brain cells as you try to understand the fine print surrounding many veterans' benefits, it's easy to lose sight of the importance of that simple, face-to-face human exchange.

Strictly speaking, even the best resume won't get you a job. The goal of a resume is to win you a job interview. Before you invest your life's savings in a professional resume-writing service, before you devote every off-duty minute of your last months in uniform polishing, tailoring, and mailing out resumes, remind yourself that the resume is an intermediate step.

The most effective use of your time and money would be to skip the intermediate step—the resume—and go directly to the job interview. Of course, it's not always possible to get a job interview by asking for one. In fact, it's usually impossible after a vacancy has been formally announced. But it's very possible between the time an employee resigns and the time a vacancy appears in the "want ads." Or even before the vacancy appears.

This is part of the process that has come to be known as "networking." Networking is a new name for something that's been going on for a long time. It happens whenever someone hears on the job about a vacancy and also knows someone outside the company who would be a strong candidate. It happens when a supervisor remembers hearing about someone with good credentials who's looking for work.

*Studies consistently show at least 60
percent of all jobs are filled through
networking.*

For most civilian workers, it's hard not to network. They know
people within their professions and throughout their communities. They know people and they're known by people. They are
networking, in a sense, every day that they're on a job.

For someone on active duty, the problems are a little different.
Usually, military people don't have professional ties to their civilian peers. Living on base, they may not even know any civilians
personally. And the community in which they plan to live after
being discharged may not be a place where they've ever actually
lived. The problems, however, have solutions.

Here are some tips for the active-duty networker:

- Stay focused on your objective. You want to learn about job
  vacancies before they are advertised. Anyone may hear about
  a vacancy, so the more people who know about your search
  the better your chances are.
- Start with people you know, then expand your network. In
  every networking discussion, you should ask for the names
  of other people you should contact. Strangers are more willing to talk to you if you can say, in the first seconds of your
  discussion, that someone they know suggested you call them.
- Keep records of names, titles, phone numbers, and dates
  when you contacted people.
- Put yourself in places where you can network. Join veterans'
  organizations, take part in community programs. Is there a
  professional organization for your career field?
- Don't overlook the people you already know on active duty,

Power-brokers must follow rules.
The lower someone is in a company,
often the better they are as a
networking contact.

especially those in the same career field. The people directly
above you in the chain of command are another source.
- See human resource and personnel departments for what
they are. They'll tell you about vacancies they're permitted
to talk about. They won't discuss likely vacancies or ones the
company wants to fill internally.
- Regardless of what anyone says, be pleasant. You're being
nice for your own sake, not theirs. You can't afford the luxury
of being testy. The longer you network, the more likely you
are to encounter someone who is rude, or even overtly hostile.
Remember that the one time you lose your cool could be
the one time that someone is testing you.
- Be brief. Many people are willing to help, but few are willing
to take on extra burdens. Don't give a networking contact
your complete life story and plans for the future. You may
also be giving them the idea that returning your phone calls
or talking to them will require a major investment of their
time.
- Keep your expectations in check. You are responsible for
your own job search. Even the most sincere, well-placed
person trying to help you might not think of you when hearing
about a vacancy. Even if a networking contact is an old family
friend who's a real power-broker in your community, don't
heave a sigh of relief and expect that person to solve your
problems. They have problems of their own that are their
first priority.

COLD FEET, COLD SHOULDERS, AND COLD CALLS

Even successful, professional salesmen are uncomfortable with "cold calls." That's their name for contacting someone "out of the blue," then trying to sell them something.

It's a lot like networking, especially the sort of long-distance networking that many military people will use to rejoin the civilian work force.

Active-duty networkers may call strangers—preferably after someone has suggested contacting them—and ask them to pass along news of vacancies.

Sales professions say you shouldn't question yourself or the value of networking if you find "cold calls" uncomfortable, even painful. There's solace in the fact that many professionals don't like them either.

7

The Ten-Step, Two-Minute Networking Phone Call

How can you network before your discharge if you are stationed hundreds of miles from the place you want to settle? An answer is to get some help from the telephone.

Here's one formula that shows what a networking conversation looks like. As a rule, it's better to call people at their place of work during regular business hours. Remember to keep a written record of names, phone numbers, addresses, and the dates of your calls.

- Introduce yourself, say you're on active duty and say that you're networking.
- Mention the name of the person who suggested you call. Or say why you're calling this person.
- Mention the specific job or field you're interested in.
- Give a five- to ten-second summary of your background. Don't go longer. Practice until you can say what needs to be said in a fraction of a minute.

- Ask if the person knows of any vacancies.
- Ask for the names of local people in your field—either supervisors or workers — whom he or she would suggest calling.
- Ask if you may send a copy of your resume, just in case he or she hears of something.
- Thank the person.
- Write a "thank you" note immediately. Especially if the person *didn't* ask for your resume. It's a way of making sure he or she has your name and address.
- Check back if the person was willing to help. Follow-up calls should come no sooner than two weeks and no later than two months.

8

A Pre-Resume, Pre-Job-Search Review

SELLING A MILITARY BACKGROUND TO A CIVILIAN WORLD

Everyone is just passing through the military. Everyone is a transient. At some point, even the longest career must end, the most decorated uniform is hung in a closet, and the most dedicated active-duty people find themselves wondering exactly what they're going to do for the rest of their professional lives.

They—and in many instances, their spouses and children, too—have sacrificed for their country. Now, many believe their country will recognize the personal cost of that service in uniform, along with the superiority of military training and the high quality of the military's management philosophy, by providing a civilian job with the paycheck, responsibility, and prestige that reflects the value of that experience on active duty.

As the vaudevillians used to say, we've got some good news, and we've got some bad news.

Knowledge is in your head.
Skills are on the workbench.
Knowledge is what you know.
Skills are what you do.
Knowledge is what you may
eventually do.
Skills are what you've already done.

The good news is that most companies are interested in hiring veterans. Desert Storm, Restore Hope, and other recent operations have put a high luster on the public image of the military. At a time when between 200,000 and 300,000 Americans file every month for unemployment for the first time, sympathy is widespread for the victims of the active-duty drawdown.

Some hire-a-vet incentives are less subtle. Many large companies keep track of the number of veterans who apply for work and the number who are hired. These programs and simple pride in the men and women in uniform help explain why veterans coming into the job market have an edge at hiring time. That's the good news.

The bad news is that most jobs go to the person who can start being productive on the first day. And the burden is on would-be employees to prove they can do that.

Consider this example. The military may have helped you get an associate degree in computer science. It may have spent hundreds of thousands of dollars to train you to repair computers and given you years of varied experiences to perfect your skills. But what happens if you apply for a civilian job that involves repairing the latest version of an IBM laptop computer? Let's say you never worked on either an IBM product or a laptop computer while on active duty.

What are your chances compared to a high-school graduate who attended a one-week course on that specific piece of equipment and who's spent a year doing nothing but IBM laptop repair? In that case, the edge goes to the less-educated, poorer-trained, less-experienced civilian.

THREE THINGS EVERY EMPLOYEE OFFERS

Keep in mind that you bring three things to a potential employer: Skills, knowledge, and traits.
- *Skills* are the things you know how to do that will get a job done. They've been formed by doing specific tasks with specific equipment.
- *Knowledge* is the information you possess that can be converted into a skill.
- *Traits* are the personal and professional qualities that affect how you work.

Employers value these three in the order in which they're listed. Skills are worth the most, since a skill matched to the right job translates into an immediate ability to be productive.

Knowledge has value, too, and often knowledge can be converted into skills with time.

Traits such as reliability and trainability are the bedrock upon which knowledge and skills can be put together to create a valuable employee.

The divisions separating skills, knowledge, and traits can be fuzzy. The deadliest gray area for the recently separated veteran is between skills and knowledge. You may be impressed by the range and depth of your knowledge about computers, but an employer may be more impressed by someone who's intimately familiar with an IBM laptop.

Armed with a general concept of skills, knowledge, and traits, you can begin considering the usefulness of your military experience to a civilian employer. Both your networking contacts and your resumes should be based upon an understanding of skills, knowledge, and traits.

Each of these three elements is important to employers, and a typical resume or networking call will touch upon all of them. But in determining how much emphasis you should put upon skills, knowledge, and traits, some rules should be kept in mind.

- Skills are more important than knowledge or traits.
- Skills are relative. To an employer who wants an IBM laptop expert, your familiarity with mainframe computers will look like knowledge, not a skill.
- Knowledge often hides a skill. If you've found yourself writing or talking about what you *know*, take another look. See if you can convert that into something you can *do*.
- The longer you've been in the work force, the less value employers tend to place upon traits. Junior officers and one-term enlisteds will get the most mileage from the personal and professional traits developed during military service.

HOW "MILITARY" SHOULD YOU BE?

Most military people are proud of what they've learned on active duty, what they've done, and how they've contributed to the nation's security.

That pride won't diminish with the years. The country's VFW and American Legion Posts are filled with gray-haired veterans who still count their service during World War II as a high point of their lives. The same will be true for the veterans who marched into Desert Storm or who stood guard during the long vigils of the Cold War.

But that pride can get in the way of being hired for a good civilian job. Even a civilian supervisor who respects the skills that people learn in uniform—a supervisor, in fact, who may also be a veteran—can be turned off by job seekers who make their resumes "too military."

There's only one job that you're certain to get with a resume littered with military jargon and titles. And that's another military job. To get a civilian job, you need to prove that you've got skills and experience that are of value to the civilian employer. Everything you learned and did on active duty can be expressed in nonmilitary language.

Often the solution is straightforward. Commanders become managers, and senior petty officers become supervisors. Marine Corps transition officials like to talk about the NCO whose last assignment was running a rifle range. There's not much demand on the civilian market for rifle-range operators. But the NCO came up with his own civilianized job title. He wrote on his resume that he had been "a facilities manager."

How much emphasis upon the military is enough? Let's look at Seven Rules for Demilitarizing Your Resume.

Rule One
If it can be expressed in civilian terms, do it. In fact, everyone should try—if only as a training exercise—to write a resume that mentions the military only in one line of the resume. That line would be something like this:

"U.S. Navy, 1989–93. Honorable discharge."

Write your own version of that line at the bottom of a piece of paper. Try filling the rest of the page with a description of your skills, experiences, accomplishments and knowledge that doesn't contain a single clue that you had ever been on active duty.

Rule Two

Convert medals into accomplishments. Were you decorated for saving the government money, improving efficiency, or upping the productivity of your military office? That's what the civilian world considers solid proof of good work, and you should get proper mileage out of it in your resume.

Describe the reason you got the medal. If need be, pull out the citation and use a key phrase or two. But keep you resume description in civilian terms. Use the phrase "officially cited for . . ." and then mention the achievement. Naming the medal is just a distraction.

Rule Three

Rule two doesn't apply to enlisted people at the end of their first enlistments or officers ending their initial obligations.

These people are young, with limited work histories, and every hiring supervisor wants some assurance that a young person is mature. For a young veteran, mentioning an end-of-tour medal can provide that assurance.

First termers should include on their resumes their highest award for individual achievement. Keep it simple and elegant. Don't go into a lot of details. A typical reference might be: "Awarded Army Commendation Medal for military service."

There are some traps here:

- Don't yield to the temptation to explain the military awards system. Yes, it's unusual for young officers to receive the Meritorious Service Medal. No, you shouldn't explain that distinction on the resume.

  An employer wants proof of your maturity, not evidence that you were a promising young officer. Few civilians are going to put you to work as a young officer, so you might as well not apply for that job.

- *Watch the flim-flam.* The National Defense Service Medal

and Southwest Asia Service Medal go, in the first instance, to those who served on active duty during the Desert Storm era, and in the second instance, to being in the Middle East during the time of Desert Storm.

Neither of those awards are for individual achievement, so don't put them down on your resume. Trying to pass those awards off as accomplishments—or claiming a decoration you didn't actually receive—won't make the difference in getting you hired. But that sort of deception, once uncovered, is guaranteed to end your employment.

Rule Four

Avoid mentioning awards for valor. Unless your application is going to a police department, fire department, or an agency of some other profession that specifically appreciates proof of heroism, decorations for valor clutter up the resume.

Instead of impressing a civilian supervisor, you may be giving him or her the idea that you're living in the past or not ready to make a complete break from the military.

Rule Five

Rule four doesn't apply to the Purple Heart. Even civilians who are ideologically opposed to military service have a soft spot for veterans who've been hurt in combat.

Again, as with so many details of your on-the-job military life, the less said in a resume the better. Don't describe your injuries or how it happened. Be straightforward and brief. You can say all you need in three words, "Purple Heart recipient."

If you use a resume format that has a major category called "Employment History," then include those three words there. Of if you use a format that has a section called "Personal," you might consider mentioning the medal there.

Rule Six

You have a civilian life, too. Your work history may have begun before you came on active duty, and your active-duty years may have included significant after-hours work in your community.

Don't look upon your resume strictly as a summary of your military skills and accomplishments. Dip into your own past. Sometimes a part-time job in high school created skills and experiences that are relevant when applying for a job years later.

Volunteer work or community work can also assume new importance during a job hunt, either for the work done or the skills gained.

Rule Seven

Don't apologize for being a civilian. Plenty of people are leaving the military these days with varying degrees of willingness.

It's natural to feel badly if you would have preferred to remain on active duty, but the Pentagon pointed you toward the door. It's natural to question yourself and to feel rejected.

But it's neither practical nor fair to yourself to carry those negative thoughts around as you look for work. So the military gave you the boot? Welcome to the club. Tens of thousands of people received the same treatment this year. Tens of thousands more in the private sector lost jobs through no fault of their own.

It's enough that you tell a hiring supervisor that your active-duty tour has ended and you have an honorable discharge. Few civilians care about the details leading up to your discharge. That applies to many hiring supervisors as well.

9

The Quick-and-Dirty Job Search

	Yes	No

Have you written chamber of commerce in new
hometown for a list of major employers?
    Contact: _____
        _____ _____ _____

Have you subscribed to Sunday newspaper in new
hometown for employment ads and housing
information?
    Contact: _____
        _____ _____ _____

Have you joined a professional association that can
help with networking?
    Contact: _____
        _____ _____ _____

Yes   No

Have you joined a veterans' organization for help in
networking and becoming a part of your new
community?
 Contact: _____
 _____   ____   ____

Is there a "headhunter" firm that specializes in
placing people with your skill and at your
professional level?
 Contact: _____
 _____   ____   ____

Is there anyone in your unit or at your base with
ties to new hometown?
 Contact: _____
 _____   ____   ____

Have you talked to a person in your career field
with more seniority than you about your civilian
job plans?
 Contact: _____
 _____   ____   ____

Have you visited the transition office for a rough
idea of their resources?
 Contact: _____
 _____   ____   ____

Notes _____
_____
_____
_____
_____
_____
_____
_____

10

Constructing Your Resume: Balloons, Building Blocks, and Sketches

The resume is a picture of your work history and skills. It's not a detailed employment record, and it's not a biography. It's not even a summary of everything you can do. It's a sketch of you that's carefully designed to appeal to a specific person, namely, a civilian supervisor with the power to hire you.

Let's be clear about what's meant by "sketch." Most shopping malls have sketch artists who appear during holidays. With a few dozen flicks of a charcoal pencil on drawing paper, they can create a simple picture that reveals a personality.

In many ways, those sketches are truer than a photograph taken of the same person at the same time. A photograph would show the shops in the background, the crowds jostling passed, perhaps even an annoyed expression that flashed across the subject's face.

The sketch, unlike the photograph, captures only the details necessary to create a clear picture of the subject. Everything else is excluded.

Anyone who's watched one of those sketch artists for a while has noticed something else. The arrangement of details in a sketch changes to fit the audience. The teenager in the varsity jacket who shows up wisecracking with his buddies may receive a sketch that makes his ears look as big as windmills, while the same ears on an elderly man might not show up at all in his sketch. The skillful artist knows when to make a joke and when to avoid offending.

There are several important truths for resume writers in the work of these sketch artists:

- Sketches don't try to depict everything.
- Sketches become clearer as you leave out irrelevant details.
- Sketches change with the audience.

These truths apply to the business of putting together a resume. Your resume should be tailored to fit the job. It should change as you learn about the needs of a certain company or even about a specific supervisor. The strength of your resume—as well as its clarity as a "sketch" of you as a worker—is determined as much by the information you leave out as the information you include.

For, in today's job market, you can't expect to bombard a supervisor with an exhaustive history of your life as an employee, expecting the supervisor to sort through it for the facts that are relevant for the present vacancy. Perhaps, in an ideal world, that's a good idea. But we don't live in an ideal world.

These days, it's quite common for a single want ad to open a floodgate, allowing dozens, perhaps even hundreds, of resumes to pour into a company. The amount of time a typical resume receives during the first, crucial screening is measured in seconds. The best that can be expected from a bulky, every-fact-I-can-think-of resume is to get tossed into a pile that will get attention

You are qualified for any job a civilian supervisor decides you're qualified for.

if a suitable candidate doesn't emerge after the first screening. That rarely happens.

When there are dozens of candidates for a job, there are always a few who know how to give a supervisor immediately the information that's being sought. That's the sort of job hunter who doesn't stay long on the unemployment lines. Usually, the "read later" pile doesn't get read.

FOCUSING ON YOUR SKILLS

For many people on active duty, writing the resume is actually the second major hurdle to cross on the road to a profitable, challenging civilian job. The first hurdle is deciding what civilian job to seek.

It's a problem with many causes. Of course, many military jobs don't have a clear-cut equivalent in the in the private sector. Even some of the noncombat jobs don't have easy counterparts in the civilian world. Many newly discharged veterans are only looking for a job near their hometown or "a good job," and it's not important to them about the career field that a job fits into.

If you're not certain about your career interests, the education office at the nearest military installation will give active-duty members aptitude tests at no cost. Spouses, retirees, dependents, and reservists may be able to take those tests at minimal cost.

Once you know what you would be interested in doing, the next task is sorting through your work history for the details that you can use to compose a sketch of yourself on a resume that will move you closer to that job.

The government will provide some help. Before their discharge, veterans are supposed to receive a form that outlines their skills, training, and experience, putting everything into civilian terms and pointing out civilian jobs that are comparable to what an individual has done on active duty.

It's called DD Form 2586, "Verification of Military Experience and Training." An example of a completed DD Form 2586 is found in the appendixes at the back of this book.

The DD Form 2586 and aptitude tests are aids. They should stimulate your thinking; they shouldn't solve your problems. They can help you answer that most difficult of life's questions, "What do I really want to be when I grow up?" But you shouldn't feel limited to the jobs or the skills in their answers. You can come up with your own.

All you need to do is convince one hiring supervisor that you're the best candidate to fill a vacancy.

THE "BALLOON METHOD" FOR RESUME WRITING AND SKILL ANALYSIS

Resumes are fearsome creatures. Even before the first word has been written on a piece of paper, we can feel cowed and threatened. Words have such power. Condensing our value as a worker into a few words is difficult and intimidating.

Fortunately, there's a time-tested way of showing a blank piece of paper who's boss. It's called doodling. During ages when people communicated on clay tablets, some scribe probably noticed that there was something about aimlessly scratching in the wet clay that helped focus and refine his thoughts.

Teachers of writing and teachers of art have long noticed the same tendency. Writing and doodling have a capacity to stimulate thought.

Resume writers can benefit from this technique. It can serve two purposes. First, it can help you discover the skills and experiences that should go into your resume. Second, it will help you shape the language that you'll be using in the resume.

Yes, it sounds crazy. But before deciding that it actually is crazy, give it a try.

The rules are simple.

- Get some paper, plus pens and pencils. *(No, you can't use your personal computer or typewriter for this writing assignment.)*
- Go to a quiet place where you know you'll have no distractions for at least a half hour.
- Write at the top of the paper, "What Have I Done?"
- Answer the question. Keep your answer to bursts of one or two words. Surround each answer with a circle, making a balloon.

An ammunition handler who tried this technique—which we'll call "the balloon method"—came up with the sketch shown in figure 1. "Explosives" and "Management" relate to two major areas of skills that he learned on active duty.

Quite wisely, the ammo handler looked at what he'd done throughout his life, not just his years on active duty. "Little League" involves an unpaid, after-duty coaching job he has done on base for a couple of summers, while "5 & 10" refers to part-time employment in the neighborhood department store before enlisting.

Figure 1 took less than a minute to complete. It didn't stay in that form for long. Our ammo handler continued on, producing the breakdown of his skills, experiences and knowledge that's shown in figure 2.

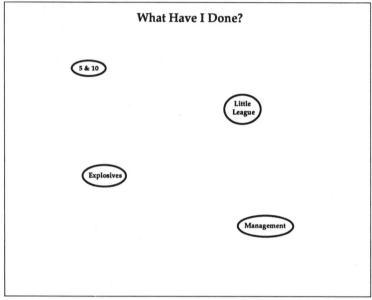

Figure 1.

Whenever a new item is related to one previously written, that relationship is shown by a line connecting two balloons.

Several things are clear so far:

- Our ammo handler has put down a mishmash of skills, experiences, ideas, job tasks, and accomplishments. Sometimes potential employers and personal traits end up inside their own balloons. That's okay.
- Many of the entries are clearly understood by an outside observer, but a few aren't. That's okay, too.
- The page is a mess. That's especially okay. The purpose of this exercise is to get ideas, not to put them into any order.

The balloon method doesn't permit the dust to gather on anyone's mental shoes. Within ten minutes, figure 2 had blossomed into figure 3, which is even more cryptic, messier and strewn

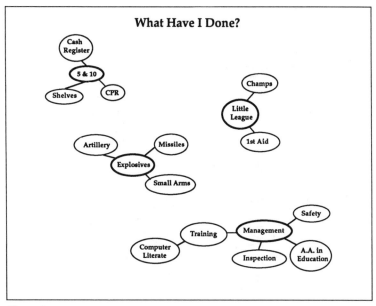

What Have I Done?

Figure 2.

with disparate elements. "Desert Storm" has joined the list of major items.

What our ammo handler has made, however, is a sketch of his working life. It was no surprise to our Ammo Handler that he'd been safety conscious during his working hours in the military, but he was surprised to realize that he'd integrated it into his Little League work. He'd even forgotten the CPR course he took while working in the five-and-dime during high school.

Using the balloon method, our ammo handler has filled one piece of paper with dozens of mental reminders about the items that should be included on a resume. In the process, our ammo handler has also been able to recall skills and experiences that had been long forgotten.

For the first time, the ammo handler saw clearly two threads

Figure 3.

running through his life—an interest in safety and an interest in kids.

No longer is our ammo handler asking, "What is an ammo handler qualified to do on the outside?"

The key question has now become: "How do I combine interests in kids and safety issues into a full-time job?"

The balloon method has helped this veteran analyze skills and break down his working experience and accomplishments into usable fragments. One more step is necessary before beginning the first resume.

BUILDING BLOCKS AND RESUMES

Sketch artists in shopping malls compose their images with a few simple, clear lines. The successful resume writer focuses on

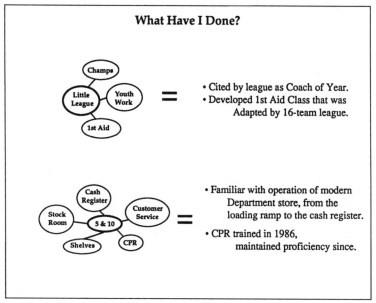

Figure 4.

another kind of line. It's the one line of simple English that best summarizes a particular skill, accomplishment, field of knowledge or interest.

As a veteran uses the balloon method to analyze both skills and work history, specific phrases will come to mind. These phrases can become the building blocks of a resume.

When our ammo handler thought of those phrases, he wrote them to one side of the piece of paper, next to the cluster of balloons with which the phrase was associated. The result looked something like figure 4.

These phrases have more details than the one- and two-word descriptions used in the balloon method. Sometimes, these phrases have relevant facts. Sometimes they show a catchy use of words, such as saying you know department store operations "from the loading ramp to the cash register."

*If it doesn't prove why you're the best
candidate for a job, it doesn't belong
in your resume.*

Initially, different people have different techniques for assembling these building blocks. Many, like our ammo handler, will wait until they've squeezed the most value from the balloon method of skill analysis before writing down any phrases. Others will jot down the phrases on the side of the piece of paper while they're still working on the balloon method.

The phrases that become resume building blocks have several features:

- They are expressed in clear, simple English.
- They are short and to the point.
- Each phrase tries to communicate only one idea, one skill, or one accomplishment.
- They contain numbers and other facts.

Those phrases are then used as building blocks, the basic materials in the construction of a resume. One resume our ammo handler might have written is shown in figure 5.

This resume follows the format known as the functional resume. The other major format, the chronological resume, uses categories based upon the jobs a person has held or the places worked.

This functional resume puts our ammo handler's skills and experiences into categories that are important to a hiring supervisor, in this case, "Safety" and "Teaching."

Into those categories, our ammo handler has placed the building blocks that show why he's the best candidate for a job. Note that the building blocks are drawn from different portions of our ammo handler's working life. Some come from active duty,

John O. Spott

1111 Polished Apple Drive
Appleton, Virginia 00000
Home: (999) 999-9999
Work: (111) 111-1111

Objective

To combine the highest government safety standards and proficiency with the latest desk-top publishing applications to create "kid-friendly" safety programs for a major public school system.

Safety

• Trained in the highest, latest standards of hazardous materials handling.
• Developed a safety program for pre-teens that was adopted for a city-wide activities program.
• Experienced in coordinating operations with law enforcement, fire safety, public health and related professionals.
• Red Cross-certified in first aid, CPR.

Teaching

• For more than a year, supervised 20-person field operation averaging 18 years of age.
• During last four years, taught an average of one safety course per quarter to classes averaging 20 young adults.
• In Little League, was cited as Coach of the Year for team that was league champions.
• Completing associate degree in education.

Employment History

• Stockboy, cashier, Hanley's Department Store, Orangeville, Wisconsin, 1987 - 1989.
• U.S. Army, 1989 - 1993. Honorable Discharge.

Personal / Technical

• Proficient with Pagemaker, Wordperfect, Lotus and Harvard Graphics.
• Awarded Army Commendation Medal for military service.
• Lifelong resident of Orangeville.

Figure 5.

some from off-duty volunteer work, and some from pre-military employment.

Each building block is there because it helps the ammo handler hit the hiring target. Even the information about computer literacy is relevant, for the veteran may be expected to produce newsletters and brochures about safety.

By using these phrases as building blocks, our ammo handler is able to tailor the resume for each job. Different phrases, for example, would show up in a resume written to seek a job in a corporate safety office or one run by a police department.

The use of building blocks helps you stay flexible. They can also serve as a sort of executive summary of your employment history. Before going to a job interview or filling out an application, review your building blocks.

They will help you remember the clearest, most direct way to tell a hiring supervisor why you're the best candidate for a job.

TIPS FOR USING THE BALLOON METHOD AND BUILDING BLOCKS

- Keep the papers on which you've tried the balloon method. A folder or spiral notebook works best.
- Once you've started looking at your employment history in terms of building blocks, you'll jot down phrases at odd moments. Keep those notes in the folder or notebook with your balloons.
- The balloon method works best in a single sitting. Don't start unless you can devote 30 minutes to an hour.
- When using the balloon method, resist the urge to organize your balloons into neat rows. Once you start organizing, the creative portion of the session is over.

- Try the balloon method to brainstorm the industries or firms that could use your skills.
- If you're not comfortable with the way you've expressed a skill or accomplishment on your resume, use the balloon method to re-analyze that particular problem.

11

Exit Bonuses and Separation Pay

Good, patriotic, valuable people are being asked to leave the military during the current drawdown. It's a unique situation for the U.S. military. For most of the twentieth century, our active-duty force has been based on draftees, and it's never been a problem to convince them to return to the private sector once the size of the military shrinks to reflect new strategic realities.

Lawmakers and Pentagon officials have struggled to come up with a package of benefits that will persuade enough people to leave active duty. The more that go voluntarily, the less likely involuntary force-outs become.

Financial incentives head the list of new inducements to hang up one's uniform. Eligible personnel can receive payments in the tens of thousands of dollars if they agree to return to the civilian world.

Attractive as these programs are, they are also very confusing. Since the get-paid-to-leave incentives are a new experience both

Check for an expiration date. Some transition benefits are scheduled to expire in 1995.

for Congress and the military, there haven't been historic lessons learned for policymakers to rely upon. They haven't known what would work and what wouldn't.

As a consequence, rules haven't been constant. Lawmakers have tinkered with the programs in each annual Defense Authorization Act passed since the incentives were created in 1990. It's reasonable to assume the tinkering will continue.

Before reviewing the details of the exit bonuses and separation pay, it's important to keep some major lessons in mind:

- Transition benefits are fluid. It's safe to assume that the following summary is a sort of baseline—a minimum list of eligibility requirements—but others may be imposed later.
- Some financial incentives may expire. When Congress created the Voluntary Separation Incentive and Special Separation Benefit, lawmakers included a provision that says the military cannot sign up people for VSI or SSB after 30 September 1995. That expiration date may change.
- For all payments, even the so-called voluntary programs, the military first decides—by rank and by career field—who will be allowed to volunteer.
- All of the payments are fully taxable. They may look like pension plan "buy-outs," which normally receive some protection from income tax, but until Congress clearly acts to give them that tax protection, they're treated at tax time like regular earned income.

VOLUNTARY SEPARATION INCENTIVE (VSI)

VSI is one of the newest acronyms to enter the military vocabulary. It stands for Voluntary Separation Incentive, one of the government's major tools for persuading people to leave active duty voluntarily.

Of course, "voluntary" is a word that may have shades of meanings. People who decline to choose the voluntary VSI payments may find themselves later tapped for an involuntary separation from active duty, with fewer benefits and less money in their pockets.

VSI has the distinction of being the most-tampered-with exit bonus. What was true last year may not be true today. But more about that below.

Amount

Like many military bonuses, VSI payments are computed using the portion of every military paycheck known as basic pay.

Other categories of pay commonly found in a military paycheck—like the quarters allowance, rations allowance, reenlistment bonuses, flight or sea pay—don't enter into the computation of VSI.

The VSI formula is simple. It involves multiplying in sequence four items: the amount of basic pay for the final month on active duty, 2.5 percent, 12, and the number of years on active duty.

The formula looks like this:

Basic pay × 0.025 × 12 × active-duty years = VSI

The years are rounded to the nearest month. Someone with eleven years and four months in uniform would be credited with 11$\frac{4}{12}$ years, or 11.3 years. (Remember to convert the fraction properly into a decimal.)

Let's look at how the formula would work in the case of an E-5 with eleven years and four months on active duty. For the sake of convenience, let's deal with round numbers and say he or she received $1,500 in basic pay during the final month in uniform. Here's how the equation would look in this case, taking each step in the formula separately.

$$\$1,500 \times 0.025 = \$37.50$$

$$\$37.50 \times 12 = \$450$$

$$\$450 \times 11.3 = \$5,085$$

So, $5,085 would be the amount of this enlisted person's VSI payment.

This isn't a one-time payment. VSI checks are sent once every year for twice the number of years on active duty. In the example above, the E-5 would receive $5,085 annually for 22 years.

The final VSI payment would include money based upon the four months—or 0.3 years—of active-duty time. That final check is calculated by multiplying the fraction of a year by the normal VSI amount. In this case, $5,085 would be multiplied by 0.3 years, yielding $1,525, which added to the normal figure of $5,085 would result in a final VSI check of $6,610.

The first VSI payment is made on a person's last day on active duty. Later payments will be made on the anniversary of that date.

People going on leave before they officially get out of the military—which is called terminal leave—can't get the first VSI check in advance.

Tax Consequences

Military people sometimes talk about VSI checks as if they are the equivalent of early, lump-sum payments from a civilian employer's pension.

Civilian workers getting early access to a pension—which is called a "lump-sum distribution"—can deposit that money into an Individual Retirement Account (IRA) within 60 days without having to pay taxes. This is called a "rollover," the transfer of money from one tax-free account to another.

Not so for VSI. The annual VSI payments are fully taxable. They are treated as if they're ordinary income.

In fact, in most cases the government will automatically withhold 20 percent of VSI payments to satisfy federal tax obligations. Or, put another way, the maximum that most VSI recipients will get is 80 percent of their payments.

Each state with an income tax has its own rules for withholdings. Generally, if money for state income taxes has been withheld from your active-duty paycheck and you live after discharge in the same state, you can count on the state getting a portion of your VSI payments before you get the money.

To make sure you understand the rules about state tax withholdings, check with the installation finance office before leaving active duty. Service members should be able to file the necessary paperwork then to increase or decrease the withholding to satisfy their tax liability.

Remember that VSI payments aren't legally a retirement. VSI recipients who live in one of the handful of states that exempt military retired pay from state taxes shouldn't expect their VSI money to be safe from state income taxes.

Still, there may be a way to reduce the tax bite. If you're legally entitled to put money into an IRA, why not make it your yearly VSI payment?

This way, a person filling out a tax form would declare the VSI as taxable income, then subtract that same amount from total income farther down the form because the money went into an IRA.

Libraries and bookstores have plenty of books that explain the finer details of IRAs. The Internal Revenue Service also publishes information. A good place to start is with the IRS booklet that every taxpayer gets explaining how to fill out the 1040 tax form.

Other Military Benefits

Recipients of VSI get more from the government than a check every year. They are also entitled to a wide range of other benefits.

A summary of the major benefits is listed below. Not included in the list are the programs available to every veteran, for which VSI recipients also qualify.

For more details about each benefit, check the appropriate chapter of this *Drawdown Survival Guide*. A summary of the major programs for veterans is included in the chapter "For All Veterans."

Here's the status of transition benefits for VSI recipients:

Access to military hospitals: *Yes, for 60 or 120 days, depending on length of service.*

CHAMPUS: *Yes, for 60 or 120 days, depending on length of service.*

Government-sponsored health insurance: *Yes. Must purchase within 30 days of discharge.*

Commissary: *Yes.*

Exchange: *Yes.*

Another chance for Montgomery GI Bill: *Yes.*

Transition counseling: *Yes. Also for spouse.*

Transition seminars: *Yes. Also for spouse.*

Access to job banks: *Yes. Also for spouse.*

Special moving, job hunting if overseas: *Yes.*

Hiring preference for civil service: *Yes, for both the transition preference and the normal veterans preference.*

Final government-paid move: *Yes. To home of record, or place entered active duty.*

Government-paid storage: *Yes. For 12 months.*

Who's Eligible

It's a little deceptive to call VSI a program to get volunteers to leave active duty. True, everyone who receives it is a volunteer. But not everyone who volunteers can get it.

The military decides who's allowed to volunteer. And volunteers aren't accepted on an individual-by-individual basis. The services will open up VSI to certain categories of active-duty people. Those categories are narrowly defined, usually in terms of rank and military skill. Each service has its own categories, and they change over time.

For example, the Army may offer VSI to diesel mechanics who are E-5s with eleven years on active duty. But an Army E-6 diesel mechanic can't get the bonus, nor can an E-5 diesel mechanic in the Navy or Air Force.

Reserve Service

VSI recipients must agree to serve in the Ready Reserve. This is a broad grouping of reservists and National Guardsmen who are assigned to units within the reserves or National Guard, or who are assigned to the manpower pool known as the Individual Ready Reserve (IRR).

They must serve in the reserves for as long as they get VSI payments.

If VSI recipients fail to attend their weekend drill periods that take place every month or their two weeks' annual training on active duty, or if they fail to perform the duties required as IRR members, then they stop getting their yearly VSI payments.

But if VSI recipients become ineligible to stay in the reserves through no fault of their own, the annual VSI payments will continue. This includes people who become too old to be in the reserves and people with medical conditions that make them unfit for reserve service.

When they receive reserve pay, there is no offsetting reduction in their VSI payments.

Government Retirements

It's no secret that the federal budget isn't a bottomless well. Rules come into play whenever people qualify to get paid twice for the same service, benefit, or disability.

Some VSI recipients will continue in the reserves long enough to earn a military retirement. Perhaps some will even end up back in uniform and qualify for an active-duty retirement.

Whatever the background, VSI recipients who earn a military retirement must repay the government for their VSI payments. The repayments begin when the retirement checks do. The repayments are made as deductions from the monthly retirement check.

Take the example of someone who receives VSI after eleven years on active duty, who then spends nine years in the reserves and so retires with twenty years of military time. The eleven years of VSI-time are 55 percent of that person's total twenty years of military time. Therefore, the government will withhold 55 percent of retirement pay until the VSI has been repaid.

(A word of caution: Trying to figure out what a withholding will look like a decade or more in the future is tricky. Don't use the current pay chart. Everyone's pay will increase, and most VSI recipients will retire at a higher rank, two factors that will shorten the repayment period.)

No interest is charged. For every dollar of VSI they receive, military retirees will repay the government with one dollar from their military retired pay.

The same dollar-for-dollar withholding takes effect when VSI recipients become eligible for disability compensation from the Department of Veterans Affairs.

VSI recipients who earn retirement benefits under the federal civil service system don't have to repay the government for their VSI checks. Like other civil service retirees, they can have the size of their retirement checks based upon their total years of federal service. Under that formula, their active-duty years are added to their civil service years.

When VSI recipients begin receiving Social Security, there is no effect upon either their Social Security or their VSI payments.

Odds and Ends
What happens to VSI payments in divorce settlements is unknown. The federal law creating VSI didn't deal with that question. Most legal experts predict VSI will be considered as community property and divided by the spouses.

Upon the death of a VSI recipient, the payments will continue to the designated beneficiary. If a veteran was eligible for fourteen years of VSI and dies five years after leaving active duty, then the official survivors will receive the annual payments for nine years.

A Little History
When Congress created the exit bonuses in 1990, fewer non-monetary benefits went to VSI recipients than to recipients of the companion bonus, the Special Separation Benefit, or SSB.

For example, originally VSI recipients were denied access to commissaries and exchanges. They were ineligible for govern-ment-paid transition medical care. Their VSI payments were reduced whenever they received pay as reservists or National Guardsmen. Even their moving allowances were less generous than the allowances given to SSB recipients.

The original inequities were quite deliberate. VSI is much larger than SSB. Lawmakers figured they could save taxpayer money in the long run by trimming the other perks that went with accepting a discharge with VSI.

But a funny thing happened on the way to the drawdown. The majority of people accepting an exit bonus during the first two years took SSB. To them, VSI, with a pay-out plan running for decades into the future, seemed too chancy. Service members were concerned that in the future Congress would change the VSI rules and deny annual payments to veterans who hadn't received all their money.

Of course, there's no way that today's Congress can provide veterans with a rock-solid guarantee that some future Congress won't cut back the benefits. To make VSI seem more desirable, lawmakers added in 1992 most of SSB's nonmonetary benefits to the VSI program.

This change has left a confusing legacy. Books and articles written before early 1993 will understate VSI benefits. Veterans and even some counselors may be unaware of some changes.

Pluses and Minuses

If a VSI recipient dies, the annual payments are unaffected. They will continue going to a spouse for the period originally promised by the government.

Some service members within a year or two of retiring from the military have elected to pick VSI and leave active duty, even though the government doesn't give involuntary discharges to people with good records and more than 18 years in uniform.

Why pass up a lifetime of retirement checks and free medical care when those benefits are only a year or two away? Here's what influenced some VSI recipients with more than 18 years in uniform:

- VSI isn't that much less than military retirement.
- VSI will continue going to a widow or widower. For retired pay to have the same protection, service members must make monthly deductions for the Survivor Benefit Plan.

- A service member may choose to live in a community where there aren't any military medical facilities.
- Some opportunities for civilian jobs won't be around in a year or two when someone qualifies for a military retirement.

Expiration Date

When Congress created the VSI program in 1990, lawmakers set up a specific expiration date. No one can sign up for VSI after 30 September 1995.

Of course, what's been written into law can be changed. Service members who are doing long-range planning with the expectation that VSI will be around in 1996 or 1997 should check whether Congress has modified the expiration date.

Highlights

- VSI is paid in yearly checks that continue for twice the number of years someone spent on active duty.
- Not everyone can volunteer for VSI. Every service member who is eligible to apply for VSI will be individually notified.
- VSI recipients don't completely walk away from the military. They must serve in the reserves.
- VSI isn't a retirement plan. For tax purposes, annual VSI payments are treated like any other kind of earned income.

SPECIAL SEPARATION BENEFIT (SSB)

SSB is another acronym that quickly became a staple of the military vocabulary. It stands for Special Separation Benefit. It's a major financial lure the Pentagon has set out to entice active-duty people into returning to the private sector.

Amount

SSB is a bonus that is based on the part of the military paycheck known as basic pay.

Other categories of pay commonly found in a military paycheck—like the quarters allowance, rations allowance, reenlistment bonuses, flight or sea pay—aren't included when figuring out SSB amounts.

The SSB formula is straightforward. It involves multiplying in sequence four items: the amount of basic pay for the final month on active duty, 15 percent, 12, and the number of years on active duty.

The formula can be expressed like this:

$$\text{Basic pay} \times 0.15 \times 12 \times \text{active-duty years} = \text{SSB}$$

The years are rounded to the nearest month. Someone with eleven years and four months in uniform would be credited with $11\frac{4}{12}$ years, or 11.3 years. (Remember to convert the fraction properly into a decimal.)

Let's look at how the formula would work in the case of an E-5 with eleven years and four months on active duty. For the sake of simplicity, let's round this service member's basic pay to $1,500 per month and take each step in the formula separately.

$$\$1,500 \times 0.15 = \$225$$

$$\$225 \times 12 = \$2,700$$

$$\$2,700 \times 11.3 = \$30,510$$

So, $30,510 would be the amount of this enlisted person's SSB payment.

And here lies a major difference between SSB and its companion payment, VSI. SSB is a one-time, lump-sum bonus. VSI is an annual payment.

That single SSB payment is made on a person's last official day on active duty.

Many people unofficially take off the uniform early by going on leave during their last days in the military. This is called terminal leave. People who take terminal leave can't get their SSB payment early. They have to wait until their last official day on active duty.

Tax Consequences

An SSB payment may look like a pension. It's often referred to as a pension. But it's not. It's fully taxable income.

Misunderstandings arise because SSB payments resemble the settlements that civilian workers receive if they leave an employer for whom they've worked many years, particularly when they've worked long enough for the employee to qualify for a pension but they're too young to begin receiving it.

In those cases, employers often will give workers a special lump-sum payment. And the workers agree to accept that single payment now instead of monthly pension checks when they reach retirement age.

The government encourages these deals—technically called "lump-sum distributions"—by offering tax protection. That money isn't subject to income taxes if it goes within 60 days into another retirement-related savings account, like an Individual Retirement Account or a Keogh Plan.

But, again, that's not the case with an SSB payment. It's treated like a regular paycheck at tax time.

In fact, it's treated like a regular paycheck when it's paid. In most cases the government will automatically withhold 20 percent of an SSB payment to satisfy federal tax obligations. Or, put another way, the maximum that most SSB recipients will get is 80 percent of the amount that's arrived at using the formula above.

Each state with an income tax has its own rules for withholdings on this kind of lump-sum payment. Generally, if money for state income taxes has been withheld from your active-duty paycheck, you can count on the state getting a portion of your SSB payment before you get the money.

To make sure you understand the rules about state tax withholdings, check with the installation finance office before leaving active duty. Service members may be able to file the necessary paperwork then to increase or decrease the withholding to satisfy their tax liability.

Remember that SSB payments aren't legally a retirement. SSB recipients who live in one of the handful of states that exempt military retired pay from state taxes shouldn't expect their SSB bonus to be safe from state income taxes.

There is, however, one way to soften the tax blow. If service members are legally entitled to put money into an IRA, they can do that with part of their SSB payment.

It won't shield the entire SSB payment from taxes. The most that single people can totally protect from taxes is $2,000. Married couples with both spouses working can shield $4,000; those with a nonworking spouse can shelter $2,250.

Those amounts can be smaller for people in certain income brackets, generally, single people earning more than $25,000 and married people with more than $40,000.

Libraries and bookstores are filled with volumes explaining the finer points about IRAs. The Internal Revenue Service also publishes information. A good place to start is with the IRS booklet that every taxpayer gets explaining how to fill out the 1040 tax form.

Other Military Benefits
SSB recipients get only one check from the government, but they are entitled to a wide range of other benefits.

The major benefits are listed below. Not included in the list are the programs available to every veteran, for which SSB recipients also qualify.

For more details about each benefit, check the appropriate chapter of this *Drawdown Survival Guide*. A summary of the major programs for veterans is included in the chapter "For All Veterans."

Here's the status of transition benefits for SSB recipients:

Access to military hospitals: *Yes, for 60 or 120 days, depending on length of service.*

CHAMPUS: *Yes, for 60 or 120 days, depending on length of service.*

Government-sponsored health insurance: *Yes. Must purchase within 30 days after end of government coverage.*

Commissary: *Yes, for two years.*

Exchange: *Yes, for two years.*

Another chance for Montgomery GI Bill: *Yes.*

Transition counseling: *Yes. Also for spouse.*

Transition seminars: *Yes. Also for spouse.*

Access to job banks: *Yes. Also for spouse.*

Special moving, job hunting if overseas: *Yes.*

Hiring preference for civil service: *Yes, for normal preference. Yes, for transition preference.*

Final government-paid move: *Yes. To home of record, or place entered active duty.*

Government-paid storage: *Yes. For one year.*

Who's Eligible

Like the VSI program, SSB payments go to volunteers. But, first, the military decides who will be allowed to volunteer.

Volunteers are accepted from certain categories of active-duty people. Those categories are strictly defined in terms of rank, military skill, and years on active duty. Each service has its own categories.

For example, the Army may offer SSB to radio operators who are E-5s with eleven years on active duty. But an E-5 radio operator for the Navy or the Air Force can't get the bonus, nor can an Army radio operator in the rank of E-6.

Since the SSB program exists solely to control the reduction in the number of people on active duty, eligible ranks and career fields will change as the services try to manage the cutback.

Reserve Service

SSB recipients must agree to spend at least three years in the Ready Reserve. This is a broad grouping of reservists and National Guardsmen who are assigned to units within the reserves or National Guard, or who are assigned to the manpower pool known as the Individual Ready Reserve (IRR).

If they fail to perform their reserve duties properly during that three-year period, then they must repay the government for the entire SSB bonus.

This includes SSB recipients expelled from the Ready Reserve for misconduct, or for failure to attend the weekend drill periods that take place every month or the two weeks' annual training on active duty.

People in the IRR who don't satisfy their obligations within the three-year period would also have to repay the government.

But, at any time, if SSB recipients become ineligible to stay in the reserves through no fault of their own, there's no repayment obligation. This includes people who become too old to be in the reserves and people with medical conditions that make them unfit for the reserves.

If SSB recipients are called to active duty, which occasionally happens for national emergencies or for individual training, there is no effect upon their SSB bonus. They keep the money.

Government Retirements

Special rules come into play whenever an SSB recipient qualifies for any federal retirement benefits. There's a jungle of government regulations designed to prevent people from getting two checks for the same time on the federal payroll.

Some SSB recipients will continue in the reserves long enough to earn a military retirement. Perhaps some will even end up back in uniform and qualify for an active-duty retirement.

Whether reservist or active-duty member, anyone who earns a military retirement must repay the government for an SSB bonus.

The repayments will be made over time as monthly deductions from retired pay. The deductions begin with the first retirement check. For every dollar of SSB they received, military retirees must repay the government with one dollar from their military retired pay. No interest is charged.

The exact formula for determining the size of the repayments is straightforward. First, figure out what percentage of total military time was the basis of the SSB bonus. Second, the government will withhold that same percentage of retired pay until SSB has been recouped.

Take the example of someone who receives SSB after eleven years on active duty, who then spends nine years in the reserves and so retires with twenty years of military time. The eleven years of SSB-time are 55 percent of that person's total twenty years of military time. Therefore, the government will withhold 55 percent of retirement pay until the SSB has been repaid.

(A word of caution: Trying to figure out what a withholding will look like a decade or more in the future is tricky. Don't use the current pay chart. Everyone's pay will increase, and most SSB recipients will retire at a higher rank, two factors that will shorten the repayment period.)

If SSB recipients become eligible for VA disability compensation, they similarly have to repay the government for the SSB payments through regular deductions from the VA disability checks.

Some SSB recipients will go on to careers in federal civil service and eventually earn a civil service retirement. Two provisions in the rule books affect them.

First, a civil service retirement isn't usually based exclusively upon the number of years in the civil service. It's based on total federal service. That means the years on active duty can be added to the years as a federal civilian to determine the amount of a civil service retirement.

To compute their civil service retirement checks, SSB recipients can claim as part of their federal service the same active-duty years upon which their SSB payment was based.

Second, there is a snag that can trip up SSB recipients. Civil servants contribute to their retirements through weekly payroll deductions. SSB recipients must do something similar to claim credit for their active-duty years when computing a civil service retirement.

Specifically, they have to contribute some money into the civil service retirement fund before they can receive a civil service retirement. The contributions will generally equal the amount of SSB.

There is, however, one way to avoid this repayment schedule. SSB recipients don't have to use their military time to qualify for a civil service retirement. If they don't claim the time, they don't have to repay the money. As a consequence, their civil service retirement checks will be smaller because they will be based on fewer years of federal service.

When SSB recipients begin receiving Social Security, there is no effect upon either their Social Security or their SSB bonus.

Odds and Ends

What happens to SSB bonuses in divorce settlements is fuzzy. The federal law creating SSB didn't deal with that question. Most legal experts predict SSB will be considered as community property and divided by the spouses.

Expiration Date

When Congress created the SSB program in 1990, lawmakers set up a specific expiration date. No one can sign up for SSB after 30 September 1995.

Of course, what's been written into law can be changed. Service members who are doing long-range planning with the expectation that SSB will be around in 1996 or 1997 should check whether Congress has modified the expiration date.

Highlights

- SSB is a one-time, lump-sum bonus. The companion benefit, VSI, is an annual payment.
- Civil servants beware! To retire in federal civil service, SSB recipients may have to repay the government for their SSB bonus.
- The SSB check comes with an obligation to spend three years in the reserves.
- SSB isn't a retirement plan. For tax purposes, the SSB payments is treated like any other kind of earned income.

SEPARATION PAY

The VSI and SSB programs are supposed to persuade people to quit the military voluntarily. But there's a third kind of bonus that's been dusted off for the drawdown, and it's called simply separation pay.

Increasingly, separation pay is being referred to as *"involuntary separation pay,"* or ISP, to distinguish it better from the two other bonuses.

Often, when transition counselors and financial officials refer to "exit bonuses," they mean only VSI and SSB. Separation pay is not officially an exit bonus.

Separation pay has been on the books for many years. It's supposed to ease the financial pain for good people whom the military decides to discharge to meet manpower limits.

Amount

The formula for determining separation pay relies on the part of the military paycheck called basic pay.

Other categories of pay commonly found in a military pay-check—like the quarters allowance, rations allowance, reenlistment bonuses, flight or sea pay—don't enter into the computation of separation pay.

Separation pay can be calculated in a few minutes. The formula involves multiplying in sequence four items: the amount of basic pay for the final month on active duty, 10 percent, 12, and the number of years on active duty.

The formula looks like this:

$$\text{Basic pay} \times 0.10 \times 12 \times \text{active-duty years} = \text{Pay}$$

The years are rounded to the nearest month. Someone with eleven years and four months in uniform would be credited with $11\frac{4}{12}$ years, or 11.3 years. (Remember to convert the fraction properly into a decimal.)

Let's look at how the formula would work in the case of an E-5 with eleven years and four months on active duty, who in round figures received $1,500 in basic pay during the final month. For the sake of simplicity, let's take each step in the formula separately.

$$\$1,500 \times 0.10 = \$150$$

$$\$150 \times 12 = \$1,800$$

$$\$1,800 \times 11.3 = \$20,340$$

So, $20,340 would be the amount of this enlisted person's separation pay.

That is, assuming the enlisted person has a good military record. For separation pay comes in two sizes—regular and half.

Half-separation pay goes to people with trouble spots on their records. (For more, see "Who's Eligible" below.) Half-separation pay is calculated using the same formula as regular separation pay, but the final number is cut in half.

Take our example of the E-5 who qualified for $20,340 in separation pay. If that enlisted member had a less-than-perfect record and qualified only for half-separation pay, that would reduce the amount to half of $20,340, or $10,170.

Whether regular sized or half-pay, separation pay is made in a single, lump-sum payment on the last day on active duty.

Many people take leave during their last days in the military. Called terminal leave, it gives them more time for moving and job hunting. But those who take terminal leave can't get their separation pay early. They have to wait until their last official day on active duty.

Tax Consequences

Separation pay is just what it says it is. It's "pay" to those "separating." It's not a pension. And that makes it fully taxable.

The tax is due when the check is made out. In most cases the government will automatically withhold 20 percent of separation pay to satisfy federal tax obligations. Or, put another way, the maximum that most people will get is 80 percent of their separation pay.

Each state with an income tax has its own rules for withholdings. Generally, if money for state income taxes has been withheld from your active-duty paycheck, you can count on the state getting a portion of your separation pay before you get the money.

To make sure you understand the rules about state tax withholdings, check with the installation finance office before leaving active duty. Service members should be able to file the necessary paperwork then to increase or decrease the withholding to satisfy their own tax liability.

Remember that separation pay isn't legally a retirement. Military people who are residents of one of the handful of states that exempt military retired pay from state taxes shouldn't expect their separation pay to be safe from state income taxes.

Some barracks lawyers argue that separation pay is just like a "lump-sum distribution," an early payment of a pension in the private sector that enjoys some protection from state and federal income taxes. Those arguments haven't changed any minds at the Internal Revenue Service.

The only tax break for recipients of separation pay are the same ones available to most taxpayers. They can shield some of the separation pay by putting it into a qualifying Individual Retirement Account or, if they're self-employed, a Keough Plan.

The most that single people can totally protect from taxes is $2,000. Married couples with both spouses working can shelter $4,000; those with a non-working spouse can shield $2,250.

Those amounts are smaller for people in higher income brackets, generally, single people earning more than $25,000 and married people with more than $40,000.

Libraries and bookstores are filled with volumes explaining the finer points of IRAs and Keough Plans. The Internal Revenue Service also publishes information. A good place to start is with the IRS booklet that every taxpayer gets explaining how to fill out the 1040 tax form.

Other Military Benefits

Although there's no single, neat definition of "involuntary separation," the people who receive separation pay come closest to experiencing the simple English meaning of the phrase.

They are good performers who are leaving active duty against their will. For them, Congress and the Pentagon have approved wide-open access to the full range of transition programs.

The major benefits are listed below. Not included in the list are the programs available to every veteran, for which separation pay recipients also qualify.

For more details about each benefit, check the appropriate chapter of this *Drawdown Update*. A summary of the major programs for veterans is included in the chapter "For All Veterans."

Here's the status of transition benefits for recipients of separation pay:

Access to military hospitals: *Yes, for 120 days.*

CHAMPUS: *Yes, for 120 days.*

Government-sponsored health insurance: *Yes. Must purchase within 30 days after end of government coverage.*

Commissary: *Yes, for two years.*

Exchange: *Yes, for two years.*

Another chance for Montgomery GI Bill: *Yes.*

Transition counseling: *Yes. Also for spouse.*

Transition seminars: *Yes. Also for spouse.*

Access to job banks: *Yes. Also for spouse.*

Special moving, job hunting if overseas: *Yes.*

Hiring preference for civil service: *Yes, for normal preference. Yes, for transition preference.*

Final government-paid move: *Yes. To any stateside home, within one year of discharge.*

Government-paid storage: *Yes, for one year.*

Who's Eligible
Separation pay is the primary bonus going to people who leave active duty involuntarily.

But there are catches and fine print. Not all people with a good record who leave the military against their will are qualified. Let's look at the details:

Full Separation Pay
Recipients must meet three broad criteria:
- They must receive honorable discharges.
- They must have at least six years on active duty, but less than twenty years.
- They must fall into one of several qualifying categories.

Those qualifying categories for full separation pay are:
- People who have been formally discharged under reduction-in-force provisions.
- Enlisted members who are fully qualified for reenlistment but denied reenlistment.
- Enlisted members rated as "fail to promote."
- Officers who are fully qualified for promotion but who are denied continuation.
- Officers rated as "non-selected for promotion."

Half-Separation Pay
Recipients must meet three broad criteria:
- They must receive discharges that are rated as honorable or general.
- They must have at least six years on active duty, but less than twenty years.
- They must fall into one of several qualifying categories.

Those qualifying categories for half-separation pay are:
- Service members judged not fully qualified for retention and therefore denied reenlistment.

- People officially discharged "for the convenience of the government."
- Everyone discharged for security reasons.
- Service members discharged for homosexuality.
- People discharged as drug rehabilitation or alcohol rehabilitation failures.
- Soldiers discharged through the Army's Qualitative Management Program (QMP).

No Separation Pay

Not eligible for either full separation pay or half-separation pay are:

- Service members who voluntarily leave active duty.
- Everyone eligible for military retirement, even if they decline to accept retired pay.
- People with less than six years on active duty.
- Service members discharged for misconduct.
- Everyone formally dropped from the rolls.
- People with dishonorable discharges, bad conduct discharges, and other-than-honorable discharges.
- Service members otherwise qualified who refuse to join the Ready Reserve.
- Everyone who declines training for a new specialty.
- People sentenced by a court-martial for discharge.
- Enlisted members at end of initial enlistment who are denied reenlistment for any reason.
- Enlisted members discharged for unsatisfactory performance.
- Officers at end of initial active-duty obligations who are denied continuation for any reason.
- Officers discharged for substandard performance.
- Reserve officers who decline a regular commission.

- Warrant officers who accept enlistment contracts.
- Reservists on active duty for training.

The first group of people on the list of those not entitled to any separation pay—"service members who voluntarily leave active duty"—deserves special emphasis.

Separation pay is for those involuntarily discharged. A military person who sees the axe coming and who decides to quit before it lands will be considered a voluntary separation, and therefore ineligible for separation pay.

In Separation Pay Limbo
When the drawdown began, service members discharged for homosexuality were given half-separation pay. Eligibility would end, of course, if the military quits discharging people for homosexuality.

Reserve Service
Just as recipients of separation pay and half-separation pay don't receive the same amount of money, they also don't incur the same obligation toward the reserves.

Those who receive the full or regular separation pay must agree to spend at least three years in the Ready Reserve. This is a broad grouping of reservists and National Guardsmen who are assigned to units within the reserves or National Guard, or who are assigned to the manpower pool known as the Individual Ready Reserve (IRR).

Those who receive half-separation pay don't have a reserve obligation. In fact, they *can't* join the reserves. The philosophy is that the same active-duty problems that made them ineligible for full separation pay also disqualify them for the reserves.

This ban includes enlisted recipients of half-separation pay who later try to qualify for officers' commissions in the reserves. It also prevents officers who got half-separation pay from entering the reserves as enlisted members.

For recipients of full separation pay, there is a financial penalty if they fail to perform their reserve duties. They must repay the government for the entire separation pay if they quit or are expelled from the reserves before finishing their three years of obligated service.

This would include people expelled from the Ready Reserve for misconduct, or for failure to attend the weekend drill periods that take place every month or the two weeks' annual training on active duty.

People in the IRR who don't satisfy their obligations within the three-year period would also have to repay the government.

At any time, if recipients of separation pay become ineligible to stay in the reserves through no fault of their own, there's no repayment obligation. This applies to people who become too old to be in the reserves and people with medical conditions that make them unfit for the reserves.

If recipients of separation pay are called to active duty, which occasionally happens for national emergencies or for individual training, there is no effect upon their separation pay. They keep the money, regardless of how long they stay on active duty.

Government Retirements

Separation pay is a government payment based upon services performed during a specific time on the government payroll.

Whenever the recipients of separation pay become eligible for another payment based upon the same period of service, something's going to happen. Usually, the recipient becomes an ex-recipient.

For example, some people who received separation pay will decide to stay in the reserves longer than their three-year obligation. They may qualify for a reserve retirement. Or perhaps they may find their way back into the active-duty rolls and qualify for an active-duty retirement.

Whether reservist or active-duty member, anyone who earns a military retirement must repay the government for separation pay.

There is a specific formula for determining the size of the repayments. First, figure out what percentage of total military time was the basis of the separation pay. Second, the government will withhold that same percentage of retired pay until the separation pay has been recouped.

Take the example of someone who receives separation pay after eleven years on active duty, who then spends nine years in the reserves and so retires with twenty years of military time. The eleven years of separation pay-time is 55 percent of that person's total twenty years of military time. Therefore, the government will withhold 55 percent of retirement pay until the separation pay has been repaid.

(A word of caution: Trying to figure out what a withholding will look like a decade or more in the future is tricky. Don't use the current pay chart. Everyone's pay will increase, and most recipients of separation pay will retire at a higher rank, two factors that will shorten the repayment period.)

No interest is charged. For every dollar of separation pay they receive, military retirees will repay the government with one dollar from their military retired pay. The repayments begin with the first retirement check.

Something similar happens if a separation pay recipient becomes eligible for VA disability pay. In some cases, that ex-service member will see a monthly reduction in the VA disability check until the government has been repaid for the full amount of separation pay.

An exception to this rule occurs when the VA disability payment is based upon injuries or disease that occurred after the active-duty period on which the separation pay is based. For example, if a recipient of separation pay became permanently disabled during the mandatory three-year period in the reserves, then that person could keep the separation pay when VA disability payments begin.

Some separation pay recipients will go on to careers in federal civil service and eventually earn a civil service retirement. They can use the active-duty years that form the basis of their separation pay in computing the size of their civil service retirement checks.

That decision, however, comes at a price. Civil service retirement checks will be reduced until the government has recouped the amount of the separation pay.

There is one way to avoid this repayment schedule. Separation pay recipients don't have to use their military time to qualify for a civil service retirement. If they don't claim the time, they don't have to repay the money. As a consequence, their civil service retirement checks will be smaller because they will be based on fewer years of federal service.

When recipients of separation pay begin receiving Social Security, there is no effect upon either their Social Security or their separation pay.

Second Chances

Some military folks who were given the chance to voluntarily hang up their uniforms—and leave active duty with VSI or SSB—later have found themselves heading toward the main gate with separation pay in their pockets.

That's a risk everyone faces when considering the option of leaving voluntarily with VSI or SSB. If you turn it down, you may not be given a second chance. What you'll be given is separation pay.

Separation pay is better than nothing. But it's smaller than either of the other two payments.

Odds and Ends
Separation pay is the subject of considerable misinformation. Strangely, that's because it's been around for a while.

VSI and SSB are new creations, programs begun specifically for the current drawdown. But separation pay has been on the books a long time. And it has undergone many changes over the years.

In fact, until November 1990, only officers could receive separation pay, and there were limits on how much they could receive.

Both the officers-only rule and the limit on the size of payments have been removed. But some careerists haven't gotten the word. Information about separation pay read from anything published before November 1990 is likely to be wrong.

Expiration Date
VSI and SSB, as originally created by Congress, were set to expire on 30 September 1995. Lawmakers may drop that date or create a new one.

Expiration isn't an issue with separation pay. The bonus has been on the books for a long time. It's scheduled to outlive the current drawdown.

Highlights
- Separation pay is a one-time, lump-sum bonus that goes to tightly defined groups of people who are discharged against their wills.
- Unlike VSI and SSB, which come in one size, separation pay comes in two sizes—regular and half.

- Recipients of the regular bonus must join the reserves. Recipients of the half-sized bonus are banned from the reserves.

VSI VERSUS SSB

It's better to get a lot of money at once, instead of getting a small but steady stream of money over a long time.

That's what many service members decide when they face the decision of choosing between the lump-sum SSB payments and the small annual income of VSI. They feel they can make more over the long term by getting a sackful of money and investing it wisely.

Can they? It's not likely.

Take the example of an E-5 with eleven years in uniform. That enlisted person would be eligible for a one-time SSB payment of $30,510. Or the E-5 could choose VSI payments of $5,085 for twenty-two years. Over the course of twenty-two years, total VSI payments will equal nearly $112,000.

That $112,000 is a lot of money, but spread out over more than two decades, won't its power be diluted? Wouldn't our E-5 end up with more money in the bank after twenty-two years by investing $30,510 at one time?

Let's examine the options. Our assumptions fit into two scenarios:

- *Scenario One:* On Discharge Day, our E-5 puts the entire SSB payment of $30,510 into a bank account at 7 percent interest.
- *Scenario Two:* On Discharge Day, our E-5 puts the initial VSI payment of $5,085 into a bank account at 7 percent interest. For the next twenty-two years, when the former E-5 receives the annual VSI check for $5,085, it goes into the same bank account, still drawing 7 percent interest.

Here's how those bank accounts would look at various periods:

	The SSB Account	*The VSI Account*
After 7 Years	$45,800	$38,900
After 12 Years	64,200	75,200
After 17 Years	90,000	136,700
After 22 Years	126,000	223,000

12

Continuing Military Benefits

Medical bills aren't a budget-breaking concern for most military families. While on active duty, they're eligible for free treatment in military hospitals and clinics.

When on-base treatment isn't available, military families can count on CHAMPUS, the Pentagon's health insurance plan, to help pay their medical bills.

Once they leave active duty, most veterans will find jobs with civilian employers who provide health insurance plans that are similar to CHAMPUS.

But it may take time to land that first job. Even after they begin work, many people will discover a gap of several months before they're covered by the employer's health plan.

And even once they're eligible for an employer's health insurance, a lot of veterans will discover that certain medical problems that arose before the hiring date—so-called pre-existing conditions—are excluded from coverage for up to a year.

To fill these gaps in medical care, Congress has authorized

the military to continue treating some people after they leave active duty.

There also is a program that allows veterans to purchase special health insurance.

ON-BASE MEDICAL FACILITIES, CHAMPUS

Military medical care is available for a few months after active duty for specific categories of people, generally the recipients of VSI, SSB, and separation pay.

The treatment available is the same that's accorded those still in uniform. That means participants can visit, free of charge, military hospitals, out-patient clinics, dental facilities, and rehabilitation clinics.

They also can continue participating in CHAMPUS, the military's health-insurance program.

Access to on-base treatment and CHAMPUS is for a fixed period of time after discharge:

- 60 days if the service member spent less than six years on active duty.
- 120 days if the service member spent six years or more on active duty.

All discharged people who qualify for on-base health care, plus their qualifying family members, receive the same priority for treatment as the dependents of active-duty people.

Remember that the 60-day and 120-day periods of care aren't for everyone with the right amounts of time in uniform. Those periods apply to people who were on active duty for those periods who also fit into one of the eligibility categories below.

Who's Eligible

At least two eligibility rules for continued medical treatment are fairly simple.

First, if the former service member is eligible for 60 or 120 days of continued medical care, so are the person's spouse, children, and anyone else in the family who meets the official definition of "dependent."

Second, if someone qualifies for this limited-period treatment in a military hospital or clinic, they're also entitled to have CHAMPUS pay some of the bills if they can't see a military doctor.

Here's the rundown on transitional medical care for recipients of the major bonuses and a few other categories of ex-service members:

VSI: *Yes.*

SSB: *Yes.*

Separation pay: *Yes.*

Half-separation pay: *Yes.*

Retire: *Not applicable. Retired status creates eligibility for full medical care.*

End-of-hitch: *No. Discharges based solely on end of obligated service don't qualify.*

VA disability: *Not applicable. Eligible for treatment in VA medical facilities.*

Other: *People who have filed for VA disability, but haven't received it yet, must seek treatment in VA facilities.*

(For more about health care available to veterans under the VA system, see the "For All Veterans" chapter.)

Odds and Ends

Some discharged veterans who are eligible for temporary treatment in a military medical facility also qualify for help from the government for so-called pre-existing conditions.

The benefit for pre-existing conditions, in most cases, involves financial help from the government to pay medical bills. Only in limited instances are people entitled to access to on-base medical facilities or to CHAMPUS beyond the 60- or 120-day limits.

Highlights
- Military medical facilities stay open after discharge for 60 to 120 days for recipients of VSI, SSB, and separation pay.
- CHAMPUS coverage also continues for these same people, with the length of coverage based on length of service and type of discharge.
- If you're eligible for one thing, you're eligible for everything. Eligible service members and their families receive access to a full range of medical services, from hospitals and dental clinics to rehabilitation services and out-patient care.

HEALTH INSURANCE

For many veterans, 60 or 120 days of additional coverage under CHAMPUS or at military medical facilities isn't enough.

To cover gaps in coverage for health care, the Pentagon negotiates with the insurance industry to find companies willing to offer short-term health insurance for veterans. Because of the Pentagon's backing, it's less expensive than most comparable plans, and it provides the range of services that veterans and their families need.

Still, it's private health insurance. In this case, "private" means it isn't free. Like any other private plan, the individual—not the government—is responsible for paying regular premiums.

What's Available
Like other private health-insurance plans, policyholders pay regular premiums to the insurance company, and in turn the company helps pay their medical bills.

Coverage is purchased in three-month blocks. Eligible people are entitled to purchase coverage for a maximum period of eighteen months.

Usually, the insurer will pick up 80 percent of approved medical expenses. Policyholders generally pay the first $250 yearly for each covered person, a payment that's called a "deductible."

If out-of-pocket expenses reach a certain level, the insurance company picks up 100 percent of the eligible expenses, up to a specified cap.

By way of comparison, in 1993 the maximum out-of-pocket expense was $2,500 yearly and the cap on total benefits was $1 million. Those figures are cited here to put costs into perspective. They are subject to change over the years.

Like any health-insurance plan, this one has a clearly defined list of services that are covered, and another equally clear list of things not covered.

Among the covered services are:
- Physicians' fees.
- Hospital rooms.
- Intensive care.
- Medical supplies, including prescription drugs.
- Ambulance and air-ambulance.
- Convalescent, nursing homes.
- Approved home care following hospitalization.

The list of services *not* covered includes:
- Routine physical examinations.
- Routine dental care.
- Injuries or illnesses covered by other plans, including Medicare, the Department of Veterans Affairs or workers' compensation.
- Eyeglasses, eye examinations.
- Induced abortions.

These lists of covered and excluded services are a summary,

and they're subject to change. The complete lists of covered and excluded services are much longer.

Military people can receive more detailed, up-to-the-minute information about coverage in information packets available at base transition offices.

Who's Eligible

Lawmakers and Pentagon officials have written the rules on health insurance to encompass the largest number of people.

Basically, everyone leaving active duty is entitled to purchase this so-called transition health insurance. Spouses and dependent children also may buy the health insurance.

Here's the rundown on health insurance for recipients of the major bonuses and a few other categories of ex-service members:

VSI: *Yes.*

SSB: *Yes.*

Separation pay: *Yes.*

Half-separation pay: *Yes.*

Retire: *Not applicable. Retired status creates eligibility for full medical care. But retirees can purchase for dependents.*

End-of-hitch: *Yes.*

Dishonorable and bad conduct discharges: *Yes.*

VA disability: *Not applicable. Eligible for treatment in VA medical facilities. But disabled veterans can purchase for dependents.*

The right of spouses and dependent children to purchase this transition health insurance isn't linked to what the ex-service member does. Spouses and children may sign up for the insurance even when ex-service members don't purchase coverage for themselves.

Rates

The cost to individuals is set by a rate table that the government negotiates with the participating insurance company. Rates are based upon three factors:

- Gender.
- Age.
- Smokers versus nonsmokers.

By way of comparison, the rates that were in effect in early 1993 started at about $240 for 29-year-old male nonsmokers, $320 for 29-year-old female nonsmokers, $270 for 29-year-old male smokers and $355 for 29-year-old female smokers.

Again, these amounts were for three months of coverage. Other rates in effect in early 1993:

- Age 34: About $265 for male nonsmokers, $400 for female nonsmokers, $290 for male smokers and $440 for female smokers.
- Age 39: About $325 for male nonsmokers, $475 for female nonsmokers, $360 for male smokers and $525 for female smokers.
- Children: About $150 per child for the first three children; no charge for additional children.

These figures are offered to provide people beginning their transition planning with an approximation of the costs of government-backed health insurance.

These rates were in effect in early 1993, and they can only be expected to increase in later years. Your transition office has the latest rates.

Applications and Deadlines

To be covered, eligible people must complete an application form and mail their first premium check to the insurance company.

Applications and initial payments must be received no later

than 30 days after the end of the 60- or 120-day period of extended governmental coverage discussed above in "On-Base Medical Facilities, CHAMPUS."

At most installations, service members will actually submit their applications and personal checks to the base personnel office. Base officials will attach the necessary information confirming eligibility before forwarding the packet to the company.

Local transition offices also have the application forms. Applications may be sent directly to the insurance company. Applications must include proof of eligibility, such as a copy of DD Form 214, a form from the Defense Enrollment Eligibility Reporting System (DEERS) or other official statement of service or dependency status.

Folks trying to sign up should remember to use an address on their application where they can be reached after discharge, not their military address.

During early 1993, the health insurance plan was provided by the Mutual of Omaha Insurance Company. It was called U.S. VIP.

PREGNANCIES AND PRE-EXISTING CONDITIONS

Like most health-insurance plans, the one backed by the government during the transition has restrictions on so-called pre-existing conditions. These are health problems that existed before someone signed up for the insurance.

The general rule is that insurance companies don't cover pre-existing conditions for new clients. There are exceptions to that rule in the transition health-insurance program.

What's a pre-existing condition? It can range from childbirth and pregnancy when the conception happened before the health-insurance policy was signed, to a bone that was broken before signing.

Technically, for transition health insurance, pre-existing conditions are illnesses or injuries that were treated within one year before the start of the health-insurance policy.

Although pregnancies are commonly listed as a pre-existing condition within the insurance industry, the military is providing medical coverage for pregnancies and childbirth under the package of transition benefits.

In short, the government will pay the normal medical expenses resulting from pregnancy and childbirth. This protection lasts for eighteen months, beginning on the date the service member's transition health-insurance policy begins.

There are some fine points about the provision for pregnancies and pre-existing conditions:

- The rules are subject to rapid change.
- The government's eighteen-month coverage for pregnancies and pre-existing conditions is for reimbursing medical bills. Eligible people aren't entitled to treatment in a military medical facility during that period.

  (There may be case-by-case and condition-by-condition exceptions. The Air Force, for example, has used base hospitals to treat pregnancies in the families of eligible ex-service members.)
- To get the eighteen-month coverage for pre-existing conditions, including pregnancies, people must purchase coverage under the transition health-insurance program.
- With the exception of pregnancies, medical services that aren't covered at any time by the health-insurance company won't be covered by the government if they're a pre-existing condition.

For example, transition health insurance doesn't provide normal dental care. Therefore, the government won't pay to fill a cavity under the rules for pre-existing conditions, even though the cavity clearly began when a person was on active duty.

Final quibble: You're not eligible for coverage for pre-existing health insurance if some other health-care program is picking up the bill for the same treatment.

Highlights

- Transition health insurance will cover the gap in health-insurance coverage that's encountered by many people after leaving the military.
- Service members pay premiums every three months for the coverage. Rates are lower than most comparable plans.
- There still are major gaps for so-called pre-existing conditions.

13

On-Base Drawdown Benefits

MILITARY ID CARD

The "ticket" of admission to most on-base services—in fact, the "ticket" of admission to most bases—is the military identification card.

Traditionally, service members, plus their spouses and children, have surrendered their ID cards on their last day on active duty.

Under rules that came into force in 1990, however, some categories of ex-service members will be given new ID cards for specific periods. That applies to spouses and children, too.

What's Available

As part of the discharge process, all service members and their spouses must still turn in their military ID cards.

The cards are formally known as DD Form 2 (for active-duty people, retirees and reservists) and DD Form 1173 (for dependents), or "Uniformed Services Identification and Privileges Card."

Each card has blocks that indicate the on-base services for which the cardholder is eligible.

Under drawdown rules, new cards will be issued to many separating service members and their families.

The transition cards will bear the stamped letters "TA" to show that the cardholder is covered by the transition assistance program.

The cards will guarantee continued access to military bases, and to their commissaries and exchanges. Markings on the card will also indicate the services not available to the bearer.

The cards will expire after two years. They cannot be renewed.

Like all military ID cards, the new "TA" cards can be confiscated by the military if the cardholder abuses privileges or fails to live up to the terms of a discharge program.

Who's Eligible

The new ID card goes to specific categories of ex-service members and their families. Many people leaving active duty won't get a card because they're not entitled to use any military services after their discharge.

As a general rule, if ex-service members are entitled to a card, so are their spouses and legal dependents.

Here's a summary of the status of ID cards for recipients of the major bonuses and a few other categories of ex-service members:

VSI: *Yes.*

SSB: *Yes.*

Separation pay: *Yes.*

Half-separation pay: *Yes.*

Retire: *Not applicable. Get ID cards as retirees.*

End-of-hitch: *No. Not unless they qualify under some other provision.*

It's important to note that people who aren't entitled to an ID card under the drawdown rules can often get one through other means, primarily by joining the reserves or the National Guard.

COMMISSARY AND EXCHANGE

The military's two major kinds of retail stores—commissaries and exchanges—will remain open for a while to certain ex-service members and their families.

What's Available

Eligible veterans and their family members can continue to shop at military commissaries and exchanges. This benefit lasts for two years after leaving active duty.

People affected by this provision will be treated in the same way as other patrons. They can visit the commissaries and exchanges as often as they like. They can buy whatever they want, subject to local restrictions affecting everyone.

Eligible people can use any commissary or exchange, even those of another military service.

The only thing that eligible people need to enter a commissary or exchange is their new "TA" military ID card. Of course, the card must indicate that they're entitled to shop in the military's retail stores.

Who's Eligible

Generally, if the ex-service member is authorized to use the commissary and exchange after discharge, so are the service member's spouse and children above the age of twelve.

Also as a general rule, access to commissaries and exchanges are linked. The people who are eligible to use a base exchange are also eligible to use the commissary.

Here's a summary of the commissary and exchange rights for

recipients of the major bonuses and a few other categories of ex-service members:

VSI: *Yes*.

SSB: *Yes*.

Separation pay: *Yes*.

Half-separation pay: *Yes*.

Retire: *Not applicable. Get full access as retirees.*

End-of-hitch: *No. Not unless they qualify under some other provision.*

ON-BASE HOUSING

Until recently, leaving the military meant packing up and going somewhere else.

Under the new drawdown rules, some ex-service members will be allowed to remain for a while in their on-base government quarters after they've been formally discharged from the military.

What's Available

Selected service members and their families can get permission to stay in on-base housing after discharge.

The limit on their stay is 180 days. That's the legal maximum. Local commanders have the authority to set limits at their bases of less than 180 days.

This isn't free housing. Participants must pay rent to the government. Usually, the rent will equal the monthly basic allowance for quarters, plus the variable housing allowance set for the area and the service member's rank.

Commanders can authorize reductions in the rent when the quarters are officially rated as substandard. Commanders also can reduce—or waive entirely—the requirement for rent in hardship cases.

Who's Eligible
The rules on eligibility are loosely drawn. Base commanders retain the final decision as to who can stay in base quarters and how long they can stay.

Still, base commanders aren't authorized to approve continued on-base housing for everyone leaving active duty during the drawdown.

Here's a summary of the housing rights for recipients of the major bonuses and a few other categories of ex-service members:

VSI: *Yes.*

SSB: *Yes.*

Separation pay: *Yes.*

Half-separation pay: *Yes*

Retire: *No.*

End-of-hitch: *No.*

While Pentagon rules give considerable latitude to base commanders to select people who'll be permitted to stay on base after discharge, the commanders also have wide authority to eject renters.

This includes cutting short periods of on-base residency that commanders had previously approved.

Applications
Check with the base housing office to find out if an installation is letting people stay in their government quarters after discharge.

Generally, if there's a waiting list for active-duty people to move into government quarters, no one should expect to stay on base after a discharge.

Odds and Ends
This is a narrowly written benefit.

It won't let someone move after discharge from one set of government quarters to another. Nor will this benefit allow a move after discharge to government quarters at another installation.

MONTGOMERY GI BILL

Since World War II, the GI Bill has helped service members and veterans continue their education.

The current version of that program, the Montgomery GI Bill, isn't as all-encompassing as its predecessors. But new drawdown rules are opening up the education benefit to thousands of people facing discharge.

What's Available

This is a contributory program. In mid-1993, service members had to give the government $100 per month from their paychecks during their first year on active duty. In return, they later get back their initial $1,200 contribution, plus at least $10,400 from the government to continue their educations.

Until recently, military people have had only one chance to sign up for the Montgomery GI Bill, and that was during their first two weeks on active duty.

But under liberalized drawdown rules, certain categories of service members who declined the Montgomery GI Bill during their early days in uniform will get a second chance.

Who's Eligible

To take advantage of the new sign-up period for the Montgomery GI Bill, military people must pass through three hoops:

- They must receive honorable discharges.
- They must meet the normal eligibility rules for the Montgomery GI Bill.
- They must fit into one of the discharge categories listed below.

The first "hoop," an honorable discharge, is straightforward.

The second "hoop," which involves meeting the normal eligibility rules for the Montgomery GI Bill, has more fine points than can be summarized here. A military education office has pamphlets outlining the basic rules.

Congress has widened this second "hoop" to include two groups normally ineligible for the education program—ROTC graduates and graduates of a service academy like West Point or Annapolis.

The third "hoop" requires would-be participants to fit into the right discharge category.

Here's a summary of whether the second chance at the Montgomery GI Bill applies to recipients of the major bonuses and a few other groups of ex-service members:

VSI: *Yes.*

SSB: *Yes.*

Separation pay: *Yes.*

Half-separation pay: *Yes, with honorable discharge.*

Retire: *No.*

End-of-hitch: *No.*

Medical disability: *Yes, under pre-drawdown rules. If separated for medical reasons, amount varies by length of service.*

Payment Schedule

Despite the easing of rules, one provision is still tough. Participants must contribute $1,200 toward the Montgomery GI Bill.

People taking advantage of the new sign-up opportunity must contribute their $1,200, in full, by the last day on active duty.

That payment may be a check written by the service member. It may also be a withholding from unused vacation that the service member was going to "cash in."

Payment may also come through monthly deductions from military pay. Service members who know in advance that they're leaving active duty and that they qualify for the Montgomery GI

Bill can instruct the government to withhold money from their paychecks.

More information about periodic withholdings can be obtained from an education, transition, or finance office.

HOUSEHOLD SHIPMENTS

When people leave active duty, they're entitled to have the government ship their household goods to their new civilian homes.

Normally, there are restrictions on where the government will pay to send furniture and personal belongings. But many of those restrictions have been lifted for certain categories of people in the drawdown.

What's Available
The last government-paid move for people leaving the military has always been handled as a regular permanent-change-of-station (PCS) move, identical to the transfers that all military people experience on active duty.

For example, both the last move and regular PCS moves are governed by the same weight restrictions on the personal property for each rank that the military will pay to ship.

What's changed for some categories of people caught in the drawdown are the places to which the government will send household goods, when the shipments can be made, and the rules for storage.

Eligible service members now can choose to ship their personal property anywhere within the United States except Alaska and Hawaii. People who came on active duty from the 49th or 50th states can have the government move their belongings back to their original civilian homes.

This last move can be made within a year of leaving active duty.

Also within that year, the government will pay to store all personal property or some of it. Then it will pay to ship the furniture and personal belongings anywhere within the 48 continental states.

The government will also pay the usual travel benefits for service members, spouses, and dependent children traveling between their last military base and their next civilian home.

Who's Eligible

Here's a summary of how the government will apply these liberalized shipping rules to recipients of the major bonuses and a few other groups of ex-service members:

VSI: *To home of record, or place entered active duty. One year's storage.*

SSB: *To home of record, or place entered active duty. One year's storage.*

Separation pay: *Liberalized shipment rules apply. One year's storage.*

Half-separation pay: *Liberalized shipment rules apply. One year's storage.*

Retire: *Not applicable. Covered by separate rules for final household goods shipment and storage.*

End-of-hitch: *Only to home of record, or place entered active duty. Limited storage.*

Retroactive

Some people who left active duty after 1 October 1990 are legally entitled to the liberalized travel and storage benefits, although the military hadn't implemented the new rules by the time those people returned to civilian life.

So retroactive travel benefits are available to some ex-service members. Eligible people are being handled differently. Some will get another government-paid move. Others will be reimbursed for certain out-of-pocket moving or storage expenses.

The retroactive moving and shipping benefits are governed by Pentagon regulations that are very specific about who's entitled to what. Officials at base offices that oversee the shipment of household goods have the full details.

DEPENDENTS' SCHOOLS

The teenaged years are tough on everyone. Lawmakers have written a provision into the drawdown rules that cushions one change for high school students.

Some students attending military-run schools overseas will be allowed to remain enrolled to graduate from high school, even after the military parent has been discharged from active duty.

What's Available

The new rules apply to qualifying military children who are enrolled in a high school operated by Department of Defense Dependents' Schools, or DoDDS.

Eligible students will be allowed to stay enrolled, free of charge, for one year to graduate. Or, put another way, they can continue their enrollment if they will graduate from high school in one year.

Students aren't entitled to attend any DoDDS school. Generally, they must go to class in the same school they attended before their military parent was discharged.

That's a general rule. Regional DoDDS directors have the authority to permit a student to attend another DoDDS school serving "the same military community."

That provision would prevent a person who had been attending a DoDDS school in Germany from switching to Italy for the final year. Still, a student should be able to switch from a school in Germany to one of the DoDDS boarding schools in England, because everyone in the military community in Germany can apply to a DoDDS boarding school in England.

Who's Eligible
Eligibility is determined by factors that affect two people—the student and the military parent.

For the student, the eligibility factors include:
- The student is an official military dependent.
- The student will have completed the junior year of high school by the time the military parent leaves active duty.
- The student is likely to graduate within 12 months after the military parent's discharge.

Also, the military parent must fall within a qualifying category for one of the parent's children to continue at DoDDS.

Here's a summary of whether this benefit applies to recipients of the major bonuses and a few other groups of ex-service members:

VSI: *Yes.*
SSB: *Yes.*
Separation pay: *Yes.*
Half-separation pay: *Yes.*
Retire: *No.*
End-of-hitch: *No.*
VA disability: *No.*

Odds and Ends
It's important to remember that the military operates two school systems for the children of active-duty people.

DoDDS serves military families overseas. Another military-run school system, the so-called Section 6 schools, educates military children at some bases in the states.

Only DoDDS students are eligible to continue in their military-run school after their parent's discharge.

Students in "Section 6" schools must enroll in a civilian school after their military parent returns to civilian life, regardless of how close they are to high school graduation.

TIME OFF

It takes time to get a job, find a home and attend to the millions of details involved in leaving the military.

Congress and the Pentagon have tried to ease the pressure by authorizing commanders to give extra time from work for people facing a discharge.

What's Available

Two specific kinds of official absences from work—excess leave and permissive temporary duty—are available to military people preparing for a return to civilian life.

Permissive temporary duty is, essentially, approval not to come into work. Under drawdown rules, commanders can approve 10 days of permissive temporary duty for service members dealing with transition-related chores.

Excess leave is vacation time beyond the 30 days of leave authorized annually for all military people. Drawdown rules let commanders approve 30 days of excess leave for separating service members.

Excess leave has to be repaid, either as time worked or as money. Anyone who owes the government for excess leave before discharge will have their final paycheck—or paychecks—docked for the amount.

The regulations specifically tell commanders to deny requests for excess leave if a service member seems unlikely to be able to repay it.

There's a further limit on availability for these two types of absences. No one can get both. Drawdown rules clearly say that commanders can approve either excess leave or permissive temporary duty for a separating service member, but not both for the same person.

Who's Eligible

Two points are crucial about eligibility for permissive temporary duty and excess leave:

- Commanders have broad authority to decide who gets how much of what.
- The time off has to be put to some transition-related purpose, like job hunting, house hunting, or attending a job-skills seminar.

There's no absolute legal right to permissive temporary duty or excess leave. The most important eligibility criterion is that an individual's commander is willing to grant the time off.

Here's a summary of whether recipients of the major bonuses and a few other groups of ex-service members are entitled to the official absences:

VSI: *Yes.*

SSB: *Yes.*

Separation pay: *Yes.*

Half-separation pay: *Yes.*

Retire: *Only ten days' permissive TDY.*

End-of-hitch: *Only ten days' permissive TDY.*

VA disability: *Only ten days' permissive TDY.*

Odds and Ends

Requests for excess leave or permissive temporary duty to attend an out-of-town class in job-hunting must meet two conditions:

- The classes can't be offered locally.
- The program must be approved by the Pentagon.

FREE SPOUSE TRAVEL

Lawmakers and Pentagon officials want everyone leaving the military to attend DoD-approved transition training programs. They want spouses to go, too.

That's difficult for many people stationed overseas, who will have to travel back to the states before their discharge dates to attend the classes.

What's Available

Spouses overseas who want to attend a transition seminar are now eligible for an increased priority for space-available travel on government aircraft.

The higher priority doesn't guarantee them a seat. But it increases the chances that they get one.

Spouses don't have to travel with their active-duty partner to take advantage of this priority.

The priority affects only overseas flights. That means:
- The flight must begin and end at overseas locations.
- Or the flight must begin overseas and end in the states.

Who's Eligible

Spouses must meet at least two conditions to qualify. First, their active-duty partner must be within 180 days of leaving active duty.

Second, the active-duty partner must be within the right category of service member. Here's a rundown on whether recipients of the major bonuses and a few other groups of ex-service members are eligible for spouse travel:

VSI: *Yes*.
SSB: *Yes*.
Separation pay: *Yes*.
Half-separation pay: *Yes*.

Retire: *No.*
End-of-hitch: *No.*
VA disability: *No.*

Odds and Ends

It's important to remember that there's a special catch in all space-available flights. The space may not be available.

Early in their planning, spouses interested in this benefit should see if it's realistic to expect to find a free seat on a government flight. They should also make sure that no other rules affect their ability to travel on a government aircraft.

RESERVE PREFERENCE

People with useful military skills are leaving active duty because of the drawdown. The military wants to hold onto as many of them as possible.

Provisions are now on the books that entitle some ex-service members to special help in getting through the door of a reserve or National Guard unit.

What's Available

Eligible veterans can receive a preference—an official edge—when reserve commanders are considering candidates for a job in a unit.

Moreover, these qualifying ex-service members can remain with a reserve unit for three years without being counted against the outfit's overall limit on manpower.

Neither the hiring preference nor the three years in special status are absolute rights. To be selected under the preference to join a unit, ex-service members have to be as qualified as the other contenders. They need good active-duty records.

And to remain three years in a unit in special status, they have to stay in good standing by fulfilling all duties and responsibilities.

Who's Eligible

To receive the preference, ex-service members must have been discharged after 1 October 1990. They also must fit within a qualifying category below.

Here's a summary of how the preference affects recipients of the major bonuses and a few other groups of ex-service members:

VSI: *Yes.*

SSB: *Yes.*

Separation pay: *Yes.*

Half-separation pay: *No. Banned from reserves.*

Retire: *No.*

End-of-hitch: *No.*

VA disability: *No. Ineligible for reserves by virtue of disability.*

Deadlines

Eligible veterans have one year after their discharge to use the hiring preference. After that period, they won't receive any special help in joining the reserves or the National Guard.

NAF PREFERENCE

Among the institutions that value the skills of people leaving the military during the drawdown are the ones that operate the services' non-appropriated funds.

The non-appropriated fund, or NAF, runs on-base programs like the exchange, officers' and enlisted clubs, theaters, and many other recreational facilities.

What's Available

Qualifying people are entitled to be considered for vacancies within the NAF personnel system.

Normally, veterans and other civilians can only apply for NAF vacancies when the personnel system can't find enough qualified candidates already on the government payroll.

Like all preferences, this is an edge at hiring time, not a guaranteed job. People using the preference are still subject to competition during the selection process.

Who's Eligible

Certain categories of ex-service members are entitled to the NAF preference. There's also a twist with this benefit.

If the ex-service member is eligible for the preference, so is the veteran's spouse.

Here's a rundown of whether recipients of the major bonuses and a few other groups of ex-service members are eligible for the preference:

VSI: *Yes.*
SSB: *Yes.*
Separation pay: *Yes.*
Half-separation pay: *Yes.*
Retire: *No.*
End-of-hitch: *No.*
VA disability: *No.*

Deadline

Eligible ex-service members and their spouses can use this preference any time after leaving active duty. There is no deadline.

While there is no deadline for using the preference, there's one other limit. Each ex-service member and spouse can use the preference only once.

Odds and Ends

This hiring edge is for NAF jobs. It doesn't apply to vacancies within the federal civil service.

14

Job-Hunting Services

PRE-SEPARATION COUNSELING

Everyone leaving active duty has always received plenty of advice about making the adjustment to civilian life.

For the drawdown, Congress has made formal counseling a matter of right. And the military has made it a priority to provide trained counselors who are aware of the latest developments in federal law and service regulations.

What's Available

The counseling sessions must address nine specific topics of interest to military people leaving active duty.

Those nine topics are spelled out in federal law. They are:
- The availability of educational assistance programs like the Montgomery GI Bill.
- A discussion of rights and procedures for disability pay and vocational rehabilitation.
- An explanation of the procedures for joining the reserves or National Guard.

- Information about job-search assistance available from the government and private sectors.
- Job-placement counseling for a service member's spouse.
- Information about governmental relocation assistance.
- Summary of medical and dental coverage after separation, including government-backed health insurance.
- Counseling on the effects of career changes upon individuals and families.
- Financial planning assistance.

Deadlines

The military will notify the service member when to report for counseling. It's supposed to occur between 90 and 180 days before the discharge date.

Active-duty people who have less than 90 days remaining before their discharge and who haven't been notified about their counseling sessions should alert their commanders about the delay.

RELOCATION ASSISTANCE

When the last assignment is overseas, service members and their families need extra help stepping back into the civilian world.

What's Available

Extra counseling about making the adjustment to the private sector is being offered to military people stationed overseas.

Service members who will be discharged overseas or discharged shortly after returning to the states are also entitled to special help in locating stateside jobs and finding a home.

The military is putting together a computerized job bank to help those overseas learn about stateside vacancies.

Who's Eligible
Relocation assistance is available to everyone leaving the military while overseas, regardless of the reason. That includes retirees, first-termers who don't want to reenlist, people leaving because of the drawdown, and those unaffected by the drawdown.

The counseling and job-search help are also available to the spouses of all service members.

Deadlines
Military people should learn about the availability of relocation assistance when they receive their pre-separation counseling, usually within 180 days of discharge.

Anyone within three or four months of discharge who hasn't been notified about the counseling sessions should alert the commander about the delay.

TRANSITION ASSISTANCE PROGRAM (TAP)

At almost all stateside installations, service members approaching discharge can attend a free, three-day seminar customized to the needs and problems of veterans returning to the private sector.

Called the Transition Assistance Program, or TAP, it's jointly sponsored by the U.S. Department of Labor, the Defense Department, and the Department of Veterans Affairs.

What's Available
TAP classes teach military job seekers exactly what they need to know—from demilitarizing a resume and translating military skills into civilian terms to learning about veterans' benefits and post-separation health care.

(For more details about the classes, see "Typical Schedule for TAP Course" in the back of this book.)

Who's Eligible

TAP classes are open to everyone about to be discharged, regardless of the reason for separation. Spouses of service members are also entitled to attend at no cost.

The classes are open to military people regardless of their parent service or place of assignment.

Deadlines and Applications

To attend, service members must be within 180 days of leaving active duty. Spouses are affected by the same time limit.

Although the program is free, reservations are needed. Interested people should try to sign up as soon as they pass the 180-day mark. Class size is limited. Some installations have been unable to fit in everyone who wants to attend.

Take the initiative. Don't wait for an official invitation to attend after you pass the 180-day mark. It often doesn't happen that way.

Leave and Travel

Service members can attend the classes without having the time deducted from their annual leave.

Absences from work must be approved by unit commanders. The Defense Department has encouraged commanders to grant the time, but they don't have to.

People stationed overseas are authorized space-available transportation back to the states to attend TAP classes. So are their spouses. But neither service members nor spouses are entitled to any reimbursements for travel, temporary lodging, or meals.

VERIFICATION OF SKILLS

In the past, veterans have had little that documents their skills and experiences in a way that was useful to civilian employers.

Beginning in 1992, that began to change.

What's Available

Active-duty people facing discharge will receive a new form that summarizes their military training and on-the-job experience.

It's called DD Form 2586, "Verification of Military Experience and Training."

It's a simple English explanation of what someone did on active duty, the training received, a description of duties, related civilian occupations, and a summary of recommended educational credit.

Many people will find the form useful in preparing their resumes. Others will want to show the document to potential employers. It doesn't take a personnel expert or a veteran to understand it.

(For a sample DD Form 2586, see "Sample Training Verification" at the back of this book.)

Who's Eligible

The form is supposed to go to everyone leaving the military, regardless of the reason, including retirees.

Deadlines and Applications

By law, the form has to be issued during the 180-day period before discharge. In practice, the military plans to begin preparing the form at the 180-day mark.

Preparation should take a couple weeks. Active-duty people should get it automatically. No applications or requests by the service member are needed.

Some delays and glitches can be expected until the form reaches widespread use. Still, people within three or four months of discharge who haven't received the form should notify their commanders.

Retroactive

Everyone discharged in 1992 and in later years has a legal right to have a DD Form 2586. Some people left active duty before the military could provide the forms.

Those people should get their forms automatically. Veterans who were discharged in 1992 and who haven't received their DD Form 2586 should contact the nearest military personnel office.

DEFENSE OUTPLACEMENT REFERRAL SYSTEM (DORS)

Among the military's drawdown-era services is a system that will offer mini-resumes to employers who tap into a computer network. This new system is called, appropriately enough, DORS (pronounced "doors").

What's Available
DORS is designed to be used by employers. When a participating company has a vacancy, its personnel officers will go to their computers and scan the mini-resumes of military people in the DORS network.

If the personnel experts see a mini-resume that looks promising, they'll contact the service member directly to request a fuller resume, or perhaps to schedule an interview.

Who's Eligible
Everyone leaving active duty, regardless of the type of discharge, is eligible to put a mini-resume into the DORS network.

Spouses of people leaving the military can also submit their mini-resumes.

Deadlines and Applications
DORS is a voluntary system. Those who want their resumes in the computerized network have to do the work to put it there.

Transition offices and family service centers have a two-page form that participants must use to summarize their training, skills, and experience.

People should fill out the applications between three and six months before they leave active duty.

Odds and Ends
Vocational counselors warn that DORS should be a small part of everyone's efforts to find a job.

COMPUTERIZED BULLETIN BOARD

The Pentagon is running another computerized network, this one to circulate news to job seekers.

Called the Transition Bulletin Board, it relies on terminals located in transition offices or family service centers.

What's Available
The bulletin board is a computerized network containing job advertisements from employers, announcements about job fairs, and updates from state employment offices.

Like DORS, it is a free service. Unlike DORS, it won't be a place where people looking for work can electronically circulate their resumes. It's strictly to publicize information useful to job seekers.

Each base will have its own policy for using the terminals. Some may permit service members to operate the equipment. Others may require a counselor to run the computer.

Who's Eligible
Everyone leaving active duty, regardless of the type of discharge, is eligible to search the transition bulletin board for information.

Spouses of people up for separation can also use it.

PROFESSIONAL CERTIFICATES

The best job search begins long before a person is out of work. And a strong tool in finding a job is a formal certificate that documents your skills.

The military has a variety of programs that offer formal certificates for training and experience. Many of these documents are recognized by unions, professional groups, and schools.

The base education office is the place to start. Education counselors can help active-duty people determine if they're eligible for any college credit or professional certification.

MILITARY ASSOCIATIONS

Members of the military community are banding together to help people affected by the drawdown. Military associations have been particularly eager to extend a hand to people looking for civilian jobs.

Efforts by most of the military associations are free and available to everyone, including non-members and people who aren't even eligible to become members.

Some typical efforts include:

- Job fairs: The Non-Commissioned Officers Association puts together regional fairs with employers and job seekers drawn from several states. Local American Legion posts sponsor smaller efforts with participants coming from the immediate communities.
- Publications: Pamphlets written specifically for military people returning to the civilian job market are a staple of the Retired Officers Association.
- Resume writing: One-on-one help in tailoring a resume for the civilian sector has been offered by the national organizations of several veterans' groups, most notably the Air Force Association and the Retired Officers Association.

- Networking, moral support: For most veterans, the most important help you will receive during your search for a worthwhile civilian job will be intangible. You establish contact with people in your new hometown who care about you. They offer tips. They keep your spirits up. It has been direct personal help such as this to veterans that has kept the doors open at local veterans' posts for decades.

Most military associations can be contacted by checking the white pages of the local telephone book. Family service centers also can help service members track down local representatives of these groups.

(For further help contacting these groups, see "National Veterans' Organizations" in the back of this book.)

15

For All Veterans

A wide variety of programs for veterans are available through many different federal and state agencies, principally the Department of Veterans Affairs, which is still commonly known by its old nickname as "the VA."

Here's a summary of the major benefits.

UNEMPLOYMENT COMPENSATION

Like many other workers who are temporarily without jobs, people who leave active duty usually qualify for weekly payments of unemployment compensation.

What's Available

Unemployment compensation is a joint program between the states and the federal government that replaces some of the income lost when people lose their jobs through no fault of their own.

The emphasis is upon the phrase "some income." It was never intended to take the place of a regular paycheck.

Each state has its own rates, with a minimum and a maximum that are based on earnings in the last job. No state's unemployment compensation is more than 50 percent of a person's former weekly earnings. Most states offer much less.

Military people should be aware of two ideas in the philosophy of unemployment compensation that are accepted by all states:

- Unemployment compensation shouldn't go to people who voluntarily leave their jobs.
- If people get lump-sum settlements of some kind as they're leaving their last full-time job, that should affect the size or duration of unemployment compensation, or even basic eligibility for the program.

Both these principles affect veterans leaving active duty. Each state will implement these two principles in its own way.

Before putting together financial plans that depend upon getting unemployment compensation, service members should discuss the specific nature of their discharge and any lump-sum payments (including unused vacation time that's "cashed in") with officials of a state employment commission.

Who's Eligible

In general terms, here's how people leaving active duty under various circumstances qualify for unemployment compensation:

End-of-hitch: All people leaving active duty because they've completed their enlistment contracts or their obligated service should be eligible for unemployment compensation in every state.

Separation pay: Veterans who receive separation pay, either the full pay or the half pay, usually qualify. The lump-sum payment, however, may delay eligibility in some states. Those states treat the lump-sum bonus as advance payment of a regular military paycheck.

VSI and SSB: Each state is still refining its policy toward recipients of these payments. Normally, unemployment compensation doesn't go to people who voluntarily leave their jobs.

Even if VSI and SSB recipients are eligible, the states also have to determine whether the payments will delay eligibility for unemployment compensation.

Early-outs: This is an "iffy" category with rapidly changing rules. States treat early-outs in different ways.

Some states may focus on the fact that folks with early-outs volunteered to leave their jobs, which makes them ineligible for unemployment compensation. Other states may emphasize that these people were about to lose their military jobs at the end of their hitches and grant the weekly payments.

Retirement: Military retirees are affected by two typical state provisions. Some states automatically declare all retirees ineligible for unemployment compensation. Others permit payments, but reduce them by the amount of retired pay.

Disability: Veterans who left active duty for medical reasons would typically have unemployment compensation offset or eliminated entirely by the amount of any disability pay.

Additionally, people with disabilities that affect their ability to work don't generally qualify for unemployment compensation.

Dishonorable, bad conduct: Another "iffy" category. A principle of unemployment compensation is that the state shouldn't support people who lost their jobs through misconduct. An adverse discharge in many states will rule out the possibility of unemployment compensation.

Other states may take a different tack, noting that veterans can receive dishonorable discharges for reasons unrelated to on-the-job performance. In these states, an adverse discharge won't close any doors to state financial help.

Odds and Ends

A few other general features of unemployment compensation are noteworthy for veterans:

- You can claim unemployment compensation in any state. That's by federal law. It doesn't have to be your home state, a state in which you ever lived, the state where you last served on active duty, or even the state in which you live after discharge.
- Don't expect a state with generous unemployment compensation to make life—or payments—easy for you if you claim unemployment compensation from them while living in another state.
- To get payments, claimants must register in person, report regularly on their efforts to get a job, and accept any work that's suitable for their skills.
- The state agencies that administer unemployment compensation also run the state's job service. These job banks are a treasure. Many employers will list vacancies only with these state agencies. The nearest office of the state job service should be a weekly stop for everyone looking for work.

REEMPLOYMENT RIGHTS

Many people who left a civilian job to come on active duty are entitled to get their old civilian jobs back, or to get an equivalent job from their former employer.

Some service members are also entitled to benefits based on seniority missed while on active duty, such as pensions, pay increases, missed promotions, and missed transfers.

These right are spelled out in the Veterans' Reemployment Rights Act.

Who's Eligible

Reemployment rights apply to people who volunteered to come on active duty, as well as those involuntarily put in uniform.

To qualify, an ex-service member has to meet five criteria. The veteran must be able to answer "Yes" to each of the five questions below. (Some of the wording that follows is awkward, but there are specific legal requirements to fulfill.)

- Before coming on active duty, you were employed in an "other than temporary" civilian job.
- You left that civilian job to go on active duty.
- You didn't stay on active duty longer than four years, unless your DD Form 214 says the time beyond the four-year mark was "at the request and for the convenience of the federal government."
- You were discharged from active duty "under honorable conditions."
- You apply for reemployment within 90 days of separating from active duty.

Appeals

Ex-service members who think an employer may be unlawfully denying them reemployment rights should contact their state's director for veterans' employment and training, often called a DVET, which is pronounced "*dee*-vet." That person works within the state's department of labor.

LIFE INSURANCE

Low-cost life insurance at group rates is offered to people leaving active duty under a plan backed by the federal government. It's called Veterans Group Life Insurance, or VGLI.

The amount of coverage is limited to the amount of Servicemen's Group Life Insurance that a person had while on active duty.

Who's Eligible
The life insurance is offered to:
- Most people who leave active duty.
- Members of the Individual Ready Reserve and the Inactive National Guard.
- Reservists who became uninsurable because of an injury sustained while serving on active duty under orders specifying they would spend less than 31 days on active duty.

Deadlines and Applications
Ex-service members must apply within 120 days of leaving active duty. Applications can be obtained from a VA office, or by writing:

Office of Servicemen's Group Life Insurance
213 Washington Street
Newark, NJ 07102

MEDICAL CARE

Hospitalization, out-patient care, nursing homes and domiciliary care are available in VA facilities to rigidly defined groups of ex-service members.

Who's Eligible
Access to VA facilities has been slowly closing over the years. Generally, the full range of VA services is now available only to the oldest or poorest veterans, or those with service-connected disabilities.

Eligibility to most services is expressed in terms of "mandatory" and "discretionary." Patients in the mandatory category *must* be

treated. Those in the discretionary category *can* be treated if space
and resources are available.

For hospital care, the mandatory category in mid-1993
included veterans who have:
- Service-connected disabilities.
- Non-service-connected disabilities, and incomes below
  about $19,000 for single people and about $23,000 for mar-
  ried people with one dependent.
- VA pensions.
- Eligibility for Medicaid.

For out-patient care, the mandatory category includes treat-
ment to veterans:
- For service-connected disabilities.
- For any disability if veteran is rated 50-percent disabled.
- For any injury suffered as a result of VA hospitalization.
- For VA-approved vocational rehabilitation.

DENTAL CARE

The full range of dental treatments, from filling cavities to major
oral surgery, is offered through VA dental facilities.

Who's Eligible

While narrowly defined groups of veterans are entitled to varying
amounts of care, all people recently discharged from active duty
qualify for one important benefit.

If service members were unable to get a routine dental examination and treatment from the military during their final months
on active duty, then those persons can go to a VA dental facility
after discharge.

Veterans must request this care at the nearest VA medical
facility within 90 days of leaving active duty. VA dentists will
refuse treatment if a veteran's separation documents show an
examination and treatment within 90 days before discharge.

DISABILITY COMPENSATION

Some veterans receive monthly VA checks to compensate them for injuries or diseases while on active duty that left them with varying disabilities.

The disabilities are rated on a scale ranging from 10 percent to 100 percent. Compensation is allocated using the same system, with people rated as 10 percent disabled receiving less than $90 monthly in 1993, while those with 100 percent disabilities receive more than $1,700.

Who's Eligible

Everyone on active duty is entitled to file a claim with VA officials for a disability.

Odds and Ends

Many transition counselors advise military members, as a part of their regular discharge process, to submit their medical records to VA review panels for a determination about eligibility.

This advice applies even—or, especially—to service members without any clear-cut handicaps.

Counselors say many medical conditions that are present in mild form at discharge may worsen over the years and entitle a veteran in later years to VA disability compensation.

By opening up a claims file with the VA as part of the separation process, while memories are fresh and medical records are still available, service members improve their chances of documenting a service connected disability decades later if a medical condition deteriorates.

16

Your Discharge Day (D-Day) Checklist

Between the decision to leave active duty and the decision to accept a specific job offer, there are an infinite number of lesser decisions.

No one can make those big decisions—or even the small, simple ones—for you. But you can be helped in identifying what needs to be decided and when you should decide. After all, you're facing your first discharge, but the military has been discharging hundreds of people every day for years. There is a lot of experience that you can learn from.

The potholes that may trip you up on your way out the main gate have already been located and marked. You don't have to start from scratch putting together a "Things to Do" list for your transition. The following pages contain a detailed schedule of places to go and people to see. Here's how to use it:

Fill in the Box

There's a box in the upper corner of every page. Underneath that box is a phrase like "180 days from D-Day." That means, 180 days before the date of your discharge. Once you know your discharge date, fill in the boxes on each page with a specific date. Do it any way you want—"Dec. 9" or "12/9"—but put a concrete date there. That's your deadline for completing the action on that page.

Write Down All the Facts

Minor details have a way of assuming major importance, and you can't predict what odd little fact will be vital to you at a later time. Make sure you collect and save basic information about your transition efforts.

Don't depend on scraps of paper. This book offers space to record those details. If you want to create your own system, use a folder or, better yet, a spiral-bound notebook.

Go in Person

Yes, you may have been in uniform since Julius Caesar was a corporal. Yes, you can get some of the information by phone. Yes, you probably can imagine what they'll tell you at the transition office. Yes, you're too busy to make pointless errands.

And, yes, you're perfectly capable of missing many of the resources that are available to people leaving active duty during the drawdown. The military is flooded with information and services related to the transition. The only sure way to find out what's available is to walk into offices and ask the people there what sort of transition help they're offering. Check bulletin boards and document racks.

Don't Be Limited by This List

Some items on this checklist are mentioned more than once. That still may not be enough for you. Improvise and add to this checklist. Especially consider becoming "a regular" at the transition center. But be cautious when it comes to deleting or sloughing off items.

When customizing your own checklist, follow some basic rules:

- Give yourself specific deadline dates.
- Write down names, titles, addresses, phone numbers, and dates.
- Get used to going places in person and talking to people. Those are keys to successful networking.

```
┌─────────────────────────────┐
│                             │
└─────────────────────────────┘
```

180 Days from D-Day

TRANSITION CENTER

Date   _____

Person Seen   _____

Address   _____

     _____

Phone   _____

Done

Pick up free literature.   _____

Locate and learn to use job banks.   _____

Locate and learn to use resume-writing computer.   _____

Check bulletin boards for free classes.   _____

Check for professional associations in your skill.   _____

Check for information about post–D-Day hometown.   _____

Make appointment to attend TAP class.   _____

Place your name in any employer data bases.   _____

Examine job-search reference books.   _____

Extra Tasks   _____

_____

_____

_____

_____

170 Days from D-Day

MEDICAL, DENTAL CHECKUPS

Before you leave active duty, the military will give you complete physical and dental examinations. That may be the last time you ever talk to a physician or dentist free of charge.

There's something even more significant about that final checkup. Upon it may hinge your ability to claim veterans' benefits years in the future for a medical problem that's only a nuisance now.

Unfortunately, for such a momentous event, the final physical and the last dental exam are often hurried, assembly-line affairs. They're not conducive to asking the medical questions you've been putting off, nor for bringing up some concern you've long brooded about, nor for requesting a specific treatment.

Take advantage of active-duty medical care while you can. Make appointments today.

Dental Appointment Date   ————————————————

Dentist   ————————————————————

Address   ————————————————————

  ————————————————————

  ————————————————————

Phone   ————————————————————

Physician Appointment Date   _____

Doctor   _____

Address   _____

_____

Phone   _____

Reminders for physician visits:

"I am often bothered physically by" _____

_____

_____

_____

"I have always wanted to ask a doctor about" _____

_____

_____

_____

_____

> *160 Days from D-Day*

EDUCATION CENTER

Date   _____

Person Seen   _____

Address   _____

  _____

Phone   _____

	Done
Verify eligibility for Montgomery GI Bill.	_____
Get literature with full details about GI Bill, including rates, rules, procedures.	_____
Check eligibility for other scholarships, loans.	_____
Check academic credit for military training.	_____
Identify schools, classes near new hometown.	_____
Check loans, scholarships for spouse.	_____
Schedule needed GED, SAT, or GRE tests.	_____
Schedule needed aptitude or interests tests.	_____
Pick up free literature.	_____
Check bulletin boards for classes, services.	_____

Extra Tasks   _____

_____

_____

---

150 Days from D-Day

LEGAL OFFICE

Date   _____

Person Seen   _____

Address   _____

              _____

Phone   _____

                                                    Done

Have personal will prepared.   _____

Create Individual Retirement Account.   _____

Discuss need for power of attorney.   _____

Discuss need for joint accounts.   _____

If receiving exit bonus, discuss tax consequences.   _____

Discuss tax status of moving expenses.   _____

Discuss tax consequences of home sale.   _____

Resolve any remaining legal problems.   _____

Pick up free literature.   _____

Check bulletin board for items of interest.   _____

Notes   _____

_____

_____

> *140 Days from D-Day*

FAMILY CENTER

Date _____

Manager _____

Address _____

_____

Phone _____

	Done
Check for transition-related classes.	_____
Check for support groups.	_____
Check for rules about post-discharge access to center and its programs.	_____
Check for babysitting services.	_____
Check for supervised programs for kids available in last weeks before discharge.	_____
Check for stress-reduction classes.	_____
Check for fun, diverting programs for you.	_____
Pick up free literature.	_____
Check bulletin boards for useful information.	_____

Notes _____

_____

_____

162 — YOUR DISCHARGE DAY (D-DAY) CHECKLIST

120 Days from D-Day

TRANSITION CENTER

Date _____

Person Seen _____

Address _____
_____

Phone _____

	Done
Check status of enrollment in TAP class.	____
Check placement in employer data bases.	____
Check availability and rules for federal jobs for spouse.	____
Check job-search services for spouse.	____
Check availability and rules for federal jobs for spouse.	____
Begin writing rough draft of your resume.	____
Begin assembling mailing list for resume.	____
Discuss job-hunting goals and strategies with a transition counselor.	____
Pick up free literature.	____
Check bulletin boards for classes, seminars.	____

Notes _____
_____
_____

> *100 Days from D-Day*

VISIT PLANNING

Even if you're planning to return after your personal D-Day to the hometown where you grew up, careful planning and a pre-discharge visit can lessen your chances of experiencing a bumpy return to the civilian world.

Here's a checklist for your visit.

Projected Date _____

Place to Stay _____

_____

_____

Phone _____

EMPLOYERS TO VISIT

Company Name _____

Person to See _____

Address _____

Phone _____

Company Name _____

Person to See _____

Address _____

Phone _____

Company Name _____

Person to See   _____

Address   _____

Phone   _____

Company Name _____

Person to See   _____

Address   _____

Phone   _____

OTHER OFFICES TO VISIT

Chamber of Commerce

Person to See   _____

Address   _____

Phone   _____

                                          Done

• Get business directory.   _____

• Get area background information.   _____

• Get cost-of-living data.   _____

• Get maps of area.   _____

Real Estate/Apartment Council

Person to See   _____

Address   _____

Phone   _____

Done

- Get data on developments, apartments.   _____

- Get maps of developments, apartments.   _____

State Employment Agency

Person to See   _____

Address   _____

Phone   _____

Done

- Get information where, when, and how to file for unemployment compensation.   _____

- Make sure you know how to operate job data bank and microfiche.   _____

- Check a few vacancies in your field.   _____

- Pick up free literature.   _____

- Check bulletin boards.   _____

Veterans' Agency

Person to See   _____

Address   _____

Phone   _____

Done

- See if medical care is available.   _____

- See if dental care is available.   _____

- See if job-hunting or counseling services are offered.   _____

- Pick up free literature.   _____

- Check bulletin boards.   _____

```
┌─────────────────────────────┐
│                             │
└─────────────────────────────┘
```

90 Days from D-Day

TRANSITION CENTER

Date _____

Person Seen _____

Address _____

_____

Phone _____

                                                          Done

Discuss latest resume with counselor.   _____

Review recent cover letter with counselor.   _____

Discuss job-search strategy with counselor.   _____

Review military and VA benefits with counselor.   _____

Discuss spouse's job search with counselor.   _____

Ask counselor for recommended reading, classes.   _____

Begin identifying "fallback" list of firms.   _____

Check data bases, computer bulletin boards.   _____

Take another look at available references.   _____

Extra Tasks _____

_____

_____

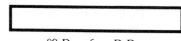

89 Days from D-Day

MORALE CHECK

Congratulations! You've just passed the halfway point. Your six-month effort to plan for an orderly, low-pain return to the private sector is more than halfway complete.

This is a good moment for taking stock. While the natural inclination is to return to the private sector like a sprinter, covering ground as quickly as possible, let's remember that your trip toward D-Day is more like a marathon. It's a long-distance haul. You don't need the quick burst of speed; you need the steady pace that you can sustain for months.

Even if you have a great job waiting for you when you walk out the main gate for the last time, you will find your resources taxed by the pressures of settling into a new home, a new job, a new life.

Check your pace. Today. Have you adopted an attitude and a schedule for your D-Day efforts that you can sustain? If you keep doing for months what you're doing today, will your brain be unfatigued, your body rested, and your spirits up? Do you believe that you're entitled to have a life now, that life isn't something that's "on hold" until after the current unpleasantness has been resolved?

Let's retake the Morale Check that appeared earlier in this book. Compare your answers today to your answers then.

THE BIG "B"— BOOZE

	Yes	*No*
Have you been drinking more alcohol, or drinking more frequently, since you began transition planning?	___	___
Have you been drunk during the last three months?	___	___
Have you failed to perform some actions for your transition because you were drunk or hung over?	___	___
Have you been arrested or been in trouble at work for situations aggravated by drinking or hangovers?	___	___
Do you believe you wouldn't drink so much if you didn't have all your current problems?	___	___
Are you uncomfortable with the amount or frequency of your drinking?	___	___

If you answered "Yes" to any question, you should consider talking to a professional about your drinking and your transition efforts. That's not to say you're an alcoholic, or even a problem drinker. But something isn't right. You are not handling the transition properly, or the transition is forcing other problems to the forefront. Make an appointment *today* with a chaplain, physician, or counselor:

Appointment Date _____

Person to See _____

Address _____

_____

_____

Phone _____

If you answered "Yes" to two questions, you should seriously consider attending a meeting of Alcoholics Anonymous. Again, you may not be an alcoholic, or even a problem drinker. But for you, drinking is getting in the way of living. Check your local telephone book *today* for the number for Alcoholics Anonymous. Call and ask for the date, time, and place of the next meeting. Show up and listen. See what they've got that you can use.

Meeting Date   ————————————————————

Meeting Time   ————————————————————

Address   ————————————————————

  ————————————————————

  ————————————————————

If you answered "Yes" to three or more questions, you've probably already wondered if booze is getting the better of you. It's starting to look that way. You need more than a quick look-see at an A.A. meeting. You need to talk personally to folks who've already faced their own problems with the bottle.

Check the local telephone book *today* for the A.A. number, then call for the date, time, and place of the next A.A. meeting. After the meeting get the telephone numbers of three people who talked during the meeting and who seemed to make sense to you. *(Yes, that means walking up to perfect strangers and asking them to help you. But give it a try. Their reactions will surprise you.)* Then call each one during the next week.

Person   ————————————————————

Phone   ————————————————————

Date to Call   ————————————————————

Person _____

Phone _____

Date to Call _____

Person _____

Phone _____

Date to Call _____

YOU'VE GOT A BODY, TOO

	Yes	*No*
Do you get your heart rate up for 20 minutes at least three times a week through exercise?	____	____
Do you break into a sweat at least three times a week?	____	____
Do you do something physical at least once a week that's fun? Something like racquetball or tennis?	____	____

A regular exercise program should be part of your transition training. It clears the mind, relaxes the body, improves the immune system, and makes you feel better. It's not a luxury you can resume after life settles down.

Leaving the military, finding a civilian job, moving to a new home and recreating life's routines is an endurance test. Exercise is one of nature's ways to build up endurance.

If you're not already exercising for at least 20 minutes on three days every week, then make exercise part of your schedule. Don't leave it to chance. Don't worry whether there are more productive things to do. Just do it.

Weekly Exercise

Day 1 _____

   Time _____

   Event _____

Day 2 _____

   Time _____

   Event _____

Day 3 _____

   Time _____

   Event _____

Weekend Special

   Day _____

   Time _____

   Event _____

DURING THE LAST WEEK . . .

	Yes	*No*
Have you seen a movie—in a theater, on TV, or on the VCR?	_____	_____
Did you have at least 30 minutes to read a book or some interesting stories from a magazine or newspaper?	_____	_____
Have you laughed out loud?	_____	_____
Have you had at least one conversation in which you could let down your guard?	_____	_____

	Yes	*No*
Has someone told you something that made you feel touched that they trusted you?	____	____
Have you talked with an elderly person?	____	____
Have you held a child?	____	____
Have you petted a dog or cat?	____	____
Have you noticed something in nature and thought, "That's pretty"?	____	____
Have you complimented at least one person every day?	____	____
Have you decided that your sex life can wait until you've straightened out your transition problems?	____	____

There are no right or wrong answers to these questions. There's only life. And these simple activities are pieces of a complete and satisfying life. Life doesn't stop while you're leaving active duty. You shouldn't allow yourself to miss any of it.

What are you going to start doing today to get a life? Put it in writing. Make a promise to yourself.

"I promise to put some life into my transition by":

_____

_____

_____

_____

A

APPENDIX:
Military Pay in Civilian Dollars

When is $1,500 worth $1,900?

It's when the $1,500 is in a monthly military paycheck, and the $1,900 is in the paycheck of a civilian worker.

A portion of each monthly military paycheck is exempt from federal, state, and Social Security taxes. The tax exemption mainly involves the housing allowances and subsistence, or rations, allowance.

This so-called tax advantage means an active-duty person takes home more money than a civilian worker who earns exactly the same amount of money.

People leaving the military must be aware of the tax advantage. If they're not, they could accept civilian jobs that seem to offer more money than they received on active duty, while actually experiencing a decrease in take-home pay.

B

APPENDIX:
Sample Training Verification

DD Form 2586 is a new job-hunting tool for ex-service members. It officially documents their on-the-job experience and their formal training.

Here's a sample of what the completed form will look like:

```
                VERIFICATION OF MILITARY EXPERIENCE AND TRAINING
```

1. LAST NAME - FIRST NAME - MIDDLE NAME	2. SEX	3. SOCIAL SECURITY NUMBER	4. PAY GRADE
John Q. Public	M	123-45-6789	E-6

5. MILITARY SERVICE AND COMPONENT	6. DATE OF BIRTH (YYMD)	7. DATE OF INFORMATION (YYMD)
Army, Active	1950 OCT 10	1991 APR 01

8. PRIMARY MILITARY OCCUPATION AND TITLE	9. YEAR(S) IN SERVICE
94B30, Food Service Specialist	13

10. EXPERIENCE AND TRAINING HISTORY (IN REVERSE CHRONOLOGICAL ORDER)

MILITARY EXPERIENCE: STAFF SERGEANT, ARMY, ACTIVE, MAR 91 - APR 91 (1 month)

SERVICE OCCUPATION(S):
    PRIMARY OCCUPATION: 94B30, Food Service Specialist , Skill Level 30
    DUTY OCCUPATION: 94B40, Food Service Specialist , Skill Level 40
    SECONDARY OCCUP: None

ADDITIONAL QUALIFICATION(S):
    None.

RELATED CIVILIAN OCCUPATION(S):
    Chef (DOT 313.131-014)
    Cook, Head, School Cafeteria (DOT 313.131-018)
    Cook (DOT 313.361-014)
    Baker (DOT 313.381-010)
    Cook, School Cafeteria (DOT 313.381-030)
    Cook (DOT 315.361-010)
    Butcher, Meat (DOT 316.681-010)
    Food-Service Supervisor (DOT 319.137-010)
    Kitchen Supervisor (DOT 319.137-030)

PRIMARY/DUTY OCCUPATION DESCRIPTION FROM AMERICAN COUNCIL ON EDUCATION (Food Service Specialist)
    Procures, prepares, and cooks food; identifies and uses appropriate equipment.
    SKILL LEVEL 10: Either has undergone on-the-job training program in food preparation and serving techniques or has recently completed a program of instruction in the basic principles of food preparation and service; under the supervision of an experienced cook, weighs, blends, mixes, and cooks food in accordance with prescribed procedures; washes, peels, cuts, and dices fruits, vegetables, meats, salads, and dairy products; prepares simple soups, sauces, and gravies; under the supervision of an experienced baker, prepares simple baked items, including breadstuffs and desserts; assists in receiving and storing food and supplies; operates and performs preventive maintenance on food service equipment; portions and serves food on serving lines; applies required sanitation procedures in handling, storing, preparing, and serving food.
    SKILL LEVEL 20: Able to perform the duties required for Skill Level 10; provides guidance to Skill Level 10 personnel; prepares meats, fruits, vegetables, salads, desserts, beverages, and dairy products for

11. ISSUING OFFICIAL	12. PAGE NUMBER
	1 of 7

Figure 6.

1. LAST NAME - FIRST NAME - MIDDLE NAME	2. SOCIAL SECURITY NUMBER	3. DATE OF INFORMATION (YYMD)
John Q. Public	123-45-6789	1991 APR 01

4. EXPERIENCE AND TRAINING HISTORY (IN REVERSE CHRONOLOGICAL ORDER)

serving; performs small-scale baking and meat cutting; operates and
performs preventive maintenance on kitchen equipment; has knowledge of
hygiene and sanitation procedures.
    SKILL LEVEL 30: Able to perform the duties required for Skill Level
20; supervises, as first cook, the scheduling of personnel and
facilities and the preparation of foods; inspects food prior to serving;
supervises procurement and storage of foods; alternative job paths are
available with assignment either as cook (leading to dining facility
manager) or as meatcutter (leading to chief meatcutter).
    SKILL LEVEL 40: Able to perform the duties required for Skill Level
30; develops work sheet according to master menu; maintains records and
files; applies accounting procedures to operate within budget; prepares
reports; serves as dining facilities manager.

AMERICAN COUNCIL ON EDUCATION CREDIT RECOMMENDATION (MOS-94B-003):
(Food Service Specialist)
    In the vocational certificate category, the recommendation is the same
as that for Skill Level 30. In the lower-division
baccalaureate/associate degree category, 6 semester hours in quantity
food preparation, 3 in kitchen operations, 3 in personnel supervision, 3
in human relations, 3 for field experience in food service, and 1 in
food service operations; IF the duty assignment was cook, 2 semester
hours in food service operations; if the duty assignment was meatcutter,
3 semester hours in meat cutting (11/77).

MILITARY EXPERIENCE: STAFF SERGEANT, ARMY, ACTIVE, MAR 90 - MAR 91 (1
year)

SERVICE OCCUPATION(S):
  PRIMARY OCCUPATION: 94B30, Food Service Specialist , Skill Level 30
  DUTY OCCUPATION: 94B20, Food Service Specialist , Skill Level 20
  SECONDARY OCCUP: None

ADDITIONAL QUALIFICATION(S):
  None.

RELATED CIVILIAN OCCUPATION(S):
  As previously stated.

PRIMARY/DUTY OCCUPATION DESCRIPTION FROM AMERICAN COUNCIL ON EDUCATION
(Food Service Specialist)
  As previously stated

MILITARY EXPERIENCE: STAFF SERGEANT, ARMY, ACTIVE, SEP 89 - MAR 90 (6
months)
----

5. INITIALS	6. PAGE NUMBER
	2 of 7

Figure 7.

```
┌────────────────────────────────────────────┬──────────────────────────┬─────────────────────────┐
│ 1. LAST NAME - FIRST NAME - MIDDLE NAME      │ 2. SOCIAL SECURITY NUMBER │ 3. DATE OF INFORMATION (YYMD) │
│                                              │                          │                         │
│ John Q. Public                               │   123-45-6789            │  1991 APR 01            │
├──────────────────────────────────────────────┴──────────────────────────┴─────────────────────────┤
│ 4. EXPERIENCE AND TRAINING HISTORY (IN REVERSE CHRONOLOGICAL ORDER)                                  │
│                                                                                                     │
│  SERVICE OCCUPATION(S):                                                                             │
│    PRIMARY OCCUPATION: 94B30, Food Service Specialist , Skill Level 30                              │
│    DUTY OCCUPATION:    94B40, Food Service Specialist , Skill Level 40                              │
│    SECONDARY OCCUP:    None                                                                          │
│                                                                                                     │
│  ADDITIONAL QUALIFICATION(S):                                                                       │
│    None.                                                                                             │
│                                                                                                     │
│  RELATED CIVILIAN OCCUPATION(S):                                                                    │
│    As previously stated.                                                                            │
│                                                                                                     │
│  PRIMARY/DUTY OCCUPATION DESCRIPTION FROM AMERICAN COUNCIL ON EDUCATION                             │
│  (Food Service Specialist)                                                                          │
│    As previously stated                                                                             │
│                                                                                                     │
│                                                                                                     │
│  MILITARY EXPERIENCE: STAFF SERGEANT, ARMY, ACTIVE, SEP 86 - SEP 89  (3                            │
│  years)                                                                                             │
│  -------------------------------------------------------------------------                         │
│                                                                                                     │
│  SERVICE OCCUPATION(S):                                                                             │
│    PRIMARY OCCUPATION: 94B30, Food Service Specialist , Skill Level 30                              │
│    DUTY OCCUPATION:    94B30, Food Service Specialist , Skill Level 30                              │
│    SECONDARY OCCUP:    None                                                                          │
│                                                                                                     │
│  ADDITIONAL QUALIFICATION(S):                                                                       │
│    None.                                                                                             │
│                                                                                                     │
│  RELATED CIVILIAN OCCUPATION(S):                                                                    │
│    As previously stated.                                                                            │
│                                                                                                     │
│  PRIMARY/DUTY OCCUPATION DESCRIPTION FROM AMERICAN COUNCIL ON EDUCATION                             │
│  (Food Service Specialist)                                                                          │
│    As previously stated                                                                             │
│                                                                                                     │
│  MILITARY EXPERIENCE: SERGEANT, ARMY, ACTIVE, SEP 85 - SEP 86  (1 year)                            │
│  -------------------------------------------------------------------------                         │
│                                                                                                     │
│  SERVICE OCCUPATION(S):                                                                             │
│    PRIMARY OCCUPATION: 94B20, Food Service Specialist , Skill Level 20                              │
│    DUTY OCCUPATION:    94B10, Food Service Specialist , Skill Level 10                              │
│    SECONDARY OCCUP:    None                                                                          │
│                                                                                                     │
│  ADDITIONAL QUALIFICATION(S):                                                                       │
│    None.                                                                                             │
│                                                                                                     │
│  RELATED CIVILIAN OCCUPATION(S):                                                                    │
│    As previously stated.                                                                            │
│                                                                          ┌──────────────┬──────────────┤
│                                                                          │ 5. INITIALS  │ 6. PAGE NUMBER │
│                                                                          │              │              │
│                                                                          │              │  3  of  7    │
└──────────────────────────────────────────────────────────────────────────┴──────────────┴──────────────┘
```

Figure 8.

1. LAST NAME - FIRST NAME - MIDDLE NAME	2. SOCIAL SECURITY NUMBER	3. DATE OF INFORMATION (YYMD)
John Q. Public	123-45-6789	1991 APR 01

4. EXPERIENCE AND TRAINING HISTORY (IN REVERSE CHRONOLOGICAL ORDER)

PRIMARY/DUTY OCCUPATION DESCRIPTION FROM AMERICAN COUNCIL ON EDUCATION
(Food Service Specialist)
  As previously stated

MILITARY EXPERIENCE: SERGEANT, ARMY, ACTIVE, SEP 84 - SEP 85 (1 year)

SERVICE OCCUPATION(S):
  PRIMARY OCCUPATION: 94B20, Food Service Specialist , Skill Level 20
  DUTY OCCUPATION: 94B30, Food Service Specialist , Skill Level 30
  SECONDARY OCCUP: None

ADDITIONAL QUALIFICATION(S):
  None.

RELATED CIVILIAN OCCUPATION(S):
  As previously stated.

PRIMARY/DUTY OCCUPATION DESCRIPTION FROM AMERICAN COUNCIL ON EDUCATION
(Food Service Specialist)
  As previously stated

MILITARY EXPERIENCE: SERGEANT, ARMY, ACTIVE, SEP 83 - SEP 84 (1 year)

SERVICE OCCUPATION(S):
  PRIMARY OCCUPATION: 94B20, Food Service Specialist , Skill Level 20
  DUTY OCCUPATION: 94B20, Food Service Specialist , Skill Level 20
  SECONDARY OCCUP: None

ADDITIONAL QUALIFICATION(S):
  None.

RELATED CIVILIAN OCCUPATION(S):
  As previously stated.

PRIMARY/DUTY OCCUPATION DESCRIPTION FROM AMERICAN COUNCIL ON EDUCATION
(Food Service Specialist)
  As previously stated

MILITARY EXPERIENCE: SERGEANT, ARMY, ACTIVE, SEP 82 - SEP 83 (1 year)

SERVICE OCCUPATION(S):
  PRIMARY OCCUPATION: 94B20, Food Service Specialist , Skill Level 20
  DUTY OCCUPATION: 94B10, Food Service Specialist , Skill Level 10
  SECONDARY OCCUP: None

5. INITIALS	6. PAGE NUMBER
	4 of 7

Figure 9.

C

APPENDIX:
Typical Schedule
for TAP Course

DAY	GENERAL	SPECIFIC	TIME
1	Introduction		2 hours
	Analyzing skills	Creating career catalogue	1 hour
	Determining values, preferences		1 hour
	Identifying needs, goals		1 hour
	Job search	Getting started	2 hours
		Dealing with stress	
		Analyzing want ads	
		Application forms	
		Researching the company	
		Employment tests	

DAY	GENERAL	SPECIFIC	TIME
2	Preparing resumes	Effective resumes Strengths, limitations of military service Translating into civilian terms	3 hours
	Writing cover letters		1/2 hour
	Interview process	Understanding it Preparing for it	1 hour
	Good grooming		1/2 hour
	Listening, responding	Sharpening skills Non-verbal cues	1/2 hour
	Asking, answering questions	Responding to the unspoken questions How to ask questions	1 1/2 hours
	Putting interview package together		1/2 hour
3	Putting interview package together		2 hours
	After interview	Following up Analyzing performance	1/2 hour
	Handling offers	Evaluating offers Negotiating Communicating decision to employer	1/2 hour
	Sources of help, vets' benefits		3 1/2 hours

D

APPENDIX: National Veterans' Organizations

NAME	HEADQUARTERS	TELEPHONE
Air Force Assoc.	Arlington, VA	(703) 247-5800
Air Force Sgts. Assoc.	Marlow Heights, MD	(301) 899-3500
American Legion	Washington, DC	(202) 861-2700
American National Red Cross	Washington, DC	(202) 737-8300
American Veterans Committee	Washington, DC	(202) 667-0090
AMVETS	Lanham, MD	(301) 459-9600
Armed Forces Communications & Electronics Assoc.	Fairfax, VA	(703) 631-6100

NAME	HEADQUARTERS	TELEPHONE
Army and Navy Union	Lakemore, OH	(216) 733-3113
Army Mutual Aid Assoc.	Arlington, VA	(703) 522-3060
Assoc. of U.S. Army	Arlington, VA	(703) 841-4300
Blinded Veterans Assoc.	Washington, DC	(202) 371-8880
Disabled American Veterans	Washington, DC	(202) 554-3501
Fleet Reserve Assoc.	Washington, DC	(202) 785-2768
Jewish War Veterans	Washington, DC	(202) 265-6280
Marine Corps League	Arlington, VA	(703) 207-9588
Marine Exec. Assoc.	McLean, VA	(703) 734-7974
Military Order of Purple Heart	Washington, DC	(703) 642-5360
National Jewish Welfare Board	New York, NY	(212) 829-3225
Navy League of U.S.	Arlington, VA	(703) 528-1775
Navy Mutual Aid Assoc.	Washington, DC	(800) 628-6011
Non-Commissioned Officers Assoc.	Alexandria, VA	(703) 549-0311
Paralyzed Veterans	Washington, DC	(202) 872-1300
Reserve Officers Assoc.	Washington, DC	(202) 479-2231
The Retired Officers Assoc.	Alexandria, VA	(703) 549-2311
Vets of Foreign Wars	Kansas City, MO	(816) 756-3390
West Point Alumni Assoc.	New York, NY	(914) 938-4600

E

APPENDIX:
State Veterans' Offices

NAME	LOCATION	TELEPHONE
Alabama: Dept. of Veterans Affairs	Montgomery, AL	(205) 242-5077
Alaska: Div. of Veterans Affairs	Juneau, AK	(907) 249-1241
American Samoa: Veterans Affairs Office	Pago Pago, American Samoa	(684) 633-4116
Arizona: Veterans Service Commission	Phoenix, AZ	(602) 255-4713
Arkansas: Dept. of Veterans Affairs	Little Rock, AR	(501) 370-3820
California: Dept. of Veterans Affairs	Sacramento, CA	(916) 445-9518
Colorado: Dept. of Social Services	Denver, CO	(303) 866-5025

NAME	LOCATION	TELEPHONE
Connecticut: Soldiers, Sailors, Marine Fund	Hartford, CT	(203) 566-2260
Delaware: Commission on Veterans Affairs	Dover, DE	(302) 739-2792
District of Columbia: Office of Veterans Affairs	Washington, DC	(202) 727-0327
Florida: Div. of Veterans Affairs	St. Petersburg, FL	(813) 898-4443
Georgia: Dept. of Veterans Services	Atlanta, GA	(404) 656-2300
Guam: Office of Veterans Affairs	Agana, Guam	(671) 472-6002
Hawaii: Office of Veterans Services	Honolulu, HI	(808) 548-8150
Idaho: Div. of Veterans Services	Boise, ID	(208) 334-5000
Illinois: Dept. of Veterans Affairs	Springfield, IL	(217) 782-6641
Indiana: Dept. of Veterans Affairs	Indianapolis, IN	(317) 232-3910
Iowa: Dept. of Public Defense	Des Moines, IA	(515) 242-5333
Kansas: Veterans Commission	Topeka, KS	(913) 296-3976
Kentucky: Div. of Veterans Affairs	Louisville, KY	(502) 564-8514
Louisiana: Dept. of Veterans Affairs	Baton Rouge, LA	(504) 342-5863
Maine: Bureau of Veterans Services	Augusta, ME	(207) 289-4060
Maryland: Veterans Service Commission	Baltimore, MD	(410) 962-4700
Massachusetts: Office of Veterans Service	Boston, MA	(617) 727-3570

NAME	LOCATION	TELEPHONE
Michigan: Veterans Trust Fund	Lansing, MI	(517) 373-3130
Minnesota: Dept. of Veterans Affairs	St. Paul, MN	(612) 296-2562
Mississippi: Veterans Affairs Board	Jackson, MS	(601) 354-7205
Missouri: Veterans Commission	Jefferson City, MO	(314) 751-3779
Montana: Veterans Affairs Division	Helena, MT	(406) 444-6926
Nebraska: Dept. of Veterans Affairs	Lincoln, NE	(402) 471-2458
Nevada: Commission of Veterans Affairs	Reno, NV	(702) 789-0155
New Hampshire: State Veterans Council	Concord, NH	(603) 624-9230
New Jersey: Div. of Veterans Service	Trenton, NJ	(609) 530-6957
New Mexico: Veterans Service Commission	Santa Fe, NM	(505) 827-6300
New York: Div. of Veterans Affairs	New York, NY	(518) 474-3752
North Carolina: Div. of Veterans Affairs	Raleigh, NC	(919) 733-3851
North Dakota: Dept. of Veterans Affairs	Fargo, ND	(701) 237-8383
Ohio: Div. of Soldiers Claims and Veterans Affairs	Columbus, OH	(614) 466-5453
Oklahoma: Dept. of Veterans Affairs	Oklahoma City, OK	(405) 521-3684
Oregon: Dept. of Veterans Affairs	Salem, OR	(503) 373-2388
Pennsylvania: Dept. of Military Affairs	Harrisburg, PA	(717) 867-8572

NAME	LOCATION	TELEPHONE
Puerto Rico: Dept. of Labor, Veterans Office	Hato Rey, PR	(809) 754-5756
Rhode Island: Veterans Affairs	Providence, RI	(401) 253-8000
South Carolina: Dept. of Veterans Affairs	Columbia, SC	(803) 734-0200
South Dakota: Div. of Veterans Affairs	Pierre, SD	(605) 773-3269
Tennessee: Dept. of Veterans Affairs	Nashville, TN	(615) 741-2345
Texas: Veterans Affairs Commission	Austin, TX	(512) 463-5538
Utah: Office of Veterans Services	Salt Lake City, UT	(801) 524-6760
Vermont: Veterans Affairs Section	Montpelier, VT	(802) 828-3379
Virginia: Div. of War Veterans Claims	Roanoke, VA	(703) 982-6396
Virgin Islands: Dept. of Veterans Affairs	Christiansted, St. Croix, Virgin Islands	(809) 773-6633
Washington: Dept. of Veterans Affairs	Olympia, WA	(206) 753-6633
West Virginia: Dept. of Veterans Affairs	Charleston, WV	(304) 348-3661
Wisconsin: Dept. of Veterans Affairs	Madison, WI	(608) 266-1315
Wyoming: Dept. of Veterans Affairs	Cheyenne, WY	(307) 778-7396

F

APPENDIX:
Drawdown Reading List

MILITARY AND VETERANS' BENEFITS

Army Times Publishing. *Handbook for the Military Family.* Springfield, Virginia, 1993. Annually updated review of everything that puts (or keeps) money in the pockets of military folks. Usually revised each April and run as an insert to regular weekly edition of *Army Times, Navy Times,* and *Air Force Times.*

U.S. Department of Defense. *Once a Veteran: The Transition to Civilian Life.* Washington, D.C., 1992. Also known as Department of Defense Pamphlet 5G [DoD PA-5G]. A readable survey of major transition programs.

U.S. Government Printing Office. *Federal Benefits for Veterans and Dependents.* Washington, D.C., 1993. A free, 100-page summary of VA services. Updated annually. Available at VA offices.

JOB HUNTING AND RESUME WRITING FOR VETERANS

Cameron, Roger. *PCS to Corporate America*. Dallas: Odenwald Press, 1990. A corporate headhunter offers advice to veterans who want to be hunted.

Fitzpatrick, William G., et al. *Does Your Resume Wear Combat Boots?* Charlottesville, Virginia: Blue Jeans Press, 1990. The snappiest title in the field. But a serious, useful treatment. Coauthor runs the top-notch job assistance program of the Non-Commissioned Officers Association.

Henderson, David G. *Job Search: Marketing Your Military Experience in the 1990s*. Mechanicsburg, Pennsylvania: Stackpole Books, 1991. One of the best, most readable and comprehensive of the drawdown books.

Jacobsen, K. C. *Retiring from Military Service*. Annapolis, Maryland: Naval Institute Press, 1990. An indispensable guide for everyone returning to the civilian job market after an absence of more than twenty years.

Lazorchak, Michael P. *The Post-Military Employment Program Workbook*. Suitland, Maryland: Airmen Memorial Foundation, 1990. Distributed by Air Force Sergeants Association. Great for figuring out what you want and how to get it.

Lee, W. Dean. *Beyond the Uniform*. New York: John Wiley & Sons, 1990. A reader-friendly treatment, also aimed at civilian servants who are back on the job market.

Nyman, Keith O. *Re-Entry: How to Turn Your Military Experience into Civilian Success*. Mechanicsburg, Pennsylvania: Stackpole Books, 1990. The basics in making the return to the private sector.

U.S. Department of Labor. *Transition Assistance Program*. Washington, D.C.: Government Printing Office, 1992. Also known as "the TAP book." Offered for attending the three-day TAP course. A fixture on the shelf of every savvy military job hunter.

AND THE BASICS . . .

Bolles, Richard Nelson. *What Color Is Your Parachute?* Berkeley, California: Ten Speed Press, 1993. The granddaddy of how-to books for the job hunter. Usually updated every year. Quirky and chock-a-block with the latest information. Not always easy reading, not always guaranteed to improve the mood of a depressed job hunter. But always determined to play straight, to be objective.

Index

Assessments
  D-Day checklists, 153–72
  emergency inventory, 3–6
  financial self-analysis, 39–42
  morale check, 17–22, 167–72
  quick-and-dirty job search,
    59–60
Associations
  addresses, 181–82
  services, 142–43

CHAMPUS, 107–16
Civil service preference, 132–34
Civil service retirement
  separation pay, 101–3
  Special Separation Benefit
    (SSB), 91–92
  VSI, 82–83
Commissaries, 119–20
Continuation, denials, 29–31

Defense outplacement (DORS),
  140–41
Dental care, 151
Dependents' schools, 126–28
Disability compensation, 152
Discharges, positive attitude
    toward, 58. *See also*
    Separation
Divorce
  and SSB, 93
  and VSI, 83

Early-outs, 25–29
Education
  dependents' schools, 126–28
  Montgomery GI Bill, 122–24
Excess leave, 128–29
Exchanges, 119–20

GI Bill, 122–24

Health insurance, 110–16
High-year of tenure, 32–33
Household shipments, 124–26
Housing, on-base, 120–22

Income tax
  military pay, 173
  SSB, 87–88
  separation pay, 95–96
  VSI, 78–80

Job search
  basics, 51–58
  quick-and-dirty, 59–60
  on-base services, 135–43

Life insurance, 149–50

Medals, 56–57
Medical care
  transition, 107–16
  VA, 150–51
Military ID card, 117–19
Military retirement
  separation pay, 101–3
  Special Separation Benefits
    (SSB), 91–92
  VSI, 82–83
Montgomery GI Bill, 122–24

NAF (non-appropriated fund) pref-
    erence, 132–33
Networking, 43–50

Permissive temporary duty (TDY),
    128–29
Promotion boards, 32–33

Reemployment rights, 148–49
Reenlistment, denials, 29–31
Relocation assistance, 136–37

Reserves
  preference, 131–32
  separation pay, 100–101
  Special Separation Benefits
    (SSB), 90
  VSI, 81–82
Resumes, 61–73
Retention, basic rules, 23–38

Selective early retirement boards
    (SERBs), 33–34
Separation
  basic rules, programs, 23–38
  counseling, 135–36
  voluntary versus involuntary,
    34–38
Separation pay
  basic rules, 31–32
  detailed rules, 93–105
Skills
  basics, 52–54
  in resume, 63–64
  verification, 138–40, 174–78
Special Separation Benefit (SSB)
  basic rules, 31–32
  detailed rules, 85–93
State veterans' offices, 183–86

Transition Assistance Program
    (TAP)
  basic rules, 137–38
  typical schedule, 179–80
Transitions, successful, 7–16
Travel, spouse, 130–31

Unemployment compensation,
    145–48

Veterans Affairs, Department of
    (VA)
  dental care, 151

disability compensation, 152
medical care, 150–51
Veterans' group life insurance,
149–50
Veterans' organizations
addresses, 181–82
services, 142–43

Voluntary Separation Incentive
(VSI)
basic rules, 31–32
detailed rules, 77–85
Voluntary versus involuntary separation, 34–38

About the Author

P. J. Budahn writes the weekly "Careers" column for the *Navy Times* family of newspapers and is a frequent contributor to *National Business Employment Weekly* on job searching, résumé writing, and military transition issues. Formerly a writer for the Peace Corps, he now works for a major veterans' organization in Washington, D. C. He lives in Springfield, Virginia.

The Naval Institute Press is the book publishing arm of the U.S. Naval Institute, a private, nonprofit society for sea service professionals and others who share an interest in naval and maritime affairs. Established in 1873 at the U.S. Naval Academy in Annapolis, Maryland, where its offices remain, today the Naval Institute has more than 100,000 members worldwide.

Members of the Naval Institute receive the influential monthly magazine *Proceedings* and discounts on fine nautical prints, ship and aircraft photos, and subscriptions to the quarterly *Naval History* magazine. They also have access to the transcripts of the Institute's Oral History Program and get discounted admission to any of the Institute-sponsored seminars offered around the country.

The Naval Institute's book-publishing program, begun in 1898 with basic guides to naval practices, has broadened its scope in recent years to include books of more general interest. Now the Naval Institute Press publishes more than sixty titles each year, ranging from how-to books on boating and navigation to battle histories, biographies, ship and aircraft guides, and novels. Institute members receive discounts on the Press's nearly 400 books in print.

Full-time students are eligible for special half-price membership rates. Life memberships are also available.

For a free catalog describing Naval Institute Press books currently available, and for further information about U.S. Naval Institute membership, please write to:

Membership & Communications Department
U.S. Naval Institute
118 Maryland Avenue
Annapolis, Maryland 21402-5035

Or call, toll-free, (800) 233-USNI.

THE NAVAL INSTITUTE PRESS

DRAWDOWN SURVIVAL GUIDE

Designed by Sandy Nadler Alberti

Set in Electra and Jay Gothic
by JDL Composition Services
Baltimore, Maryland

Printed on 50-lb. Domtar Windsor offset smooth white
and bound by John D. Lucas Printing
Baltimore, Maryland